1st EDITION

Perspectives on Diseases and Disorders

Muscular Dystrophy

Clay Farris Naff
Book Editor

PERSPECTIVES
On Diseases & Disorders

GALE
CENGAGE Learning·

Detroit • New York • San Francisco • New Haven, Conn • Waterville, Maine • London

Elizabeth Des Chenes, *Managing Editor*

Articles in Greenhaven Press anthologies are often edited for length to meet page requirements. In addition, original titles of these works are changed to clearly present the main thesis and to explicitly indicate the author's opinion. Every effort is made to ensure that Greenhaven Press accurately reflects the original intent of the authors. Every effort has been made to trace the owners of copyrighted material.

Cover image © Huntstock, Inc./Phototake. All rights reserved.

LIBRARY OF CONGRESS CATALOGING-IN-PUBLICATION DATA

Muscular dystrophy / Clay Farris Naff, Book Editor.
  p. cm. -- (Perspectives on diseases and disorders)
 Includes bibliographical references and index.
 ISBN 978-0-7377-5780-4 (hardcover)
 1. Muscular dystrophy--Juvenile literature. I. Naff, Clay Farris.
 RC935.M7M867 2011
 616.7'48--dc23
                                                          2011024262

Printed in the United States of America
1 2 3 4 5 6 7 15 14 13 12 11

CONTENTS

Foreword   7

Introduction   9

CHAPTER 1   **Understanding Muscular Dystrophy**

1. An Overview of Muscular Dystrophy   15

Nada Quercia

Muscular dystrophy, a genetic disease that breaks down the lines of communication between the brain and muscles, can be understood as a complex of many diseases.

2. National Programs Aim to Understand and Treat Muscular Dystrophy   29

National Institutes of Health

The Muscular Dystrophy Community Assistance, Research, and Education Act ensures the expansion and intensification of muscular dystrophy research. Diverse institutes and centers currently have programs addressing the disease under way.

3. A New Technique May Aid in Diagnosis of Muscular Dystrophy   41

Heather Hare

Diagnoses of Duchenne muscular dystrophy are often unnecessarily delayed. Now, however, a simple blood test for enzyme levels may speed diagnosis.

4. Scientists Are Closing In on the Genes
   That Cause Muscular Dystrophy   45

Tom Rickey

Members of an international team of scientists
believe they have identified the defective genes
that lead to muscular dystrophy.

5. Drug Therapy Gives Cautious Optimism for
   Treating Muscular Dystrophy   51

Matthew Herper

An experimental drug is associated with
improvement in some muscular dystrophy
patients; however, a history of disappointments
attempting to treat the disease with drug therapy
has scientists remaining cautiously optimistic.

6. A Popular Nutritional Supplement May Aid
   in Treatment of Muscular Dystrophy   56

Jared P. Pearlman and Roger A. Fielding

Creatine, made famous as a muscle-building
nutritional supplement in the 1990s by Major
League home-run champion Mark McGwire,
may have a role in treating muscular dystrophy;
however, its reputation may stand in the way of
its acceptance.

CHAPTER 2   Issues and Controversies Concerning
             Muscular Dystrophy

1. Stem Cell Therapy Has Not Produced Cures
   for Diseases Such as Muscular Dystrophy   65

Emily Yoffe

Despite high hopes, stem cell research has yet to
produce safe, reliable cures. Muscular dystrophy
patients, whose hopes have been particularly
stimulated by this research, have thus far been
disappointed.

2. Gene Therapy Offers Hopeful Treatment
   Possibilities for Muscular Dystrophy   72

   Amanda Gardner

   The age of gene therapy for treating muscular
   dystrophy may have dawned. Scientists have
   successfully made use of injected genes to
   help MD patients improve. The prospects are
   promising.

3. Gene Therapy Has Challenges to
   Overcome Before It Can Effectively
   Treat Muscular Dystrophy   76

   Nationwide Children's Hospital

   Gene therapy may become useful for treating
   MD, but many challenges stand in the way,
   including a safe and effective means to transport
   reparative genes into the patient's cells.

4. Trials Fail to Prove Ataluren as Effective
   for Treating Muscular Dystrophy   82

   Quest Magazine

   A pharmaceutical company dampens excitement
   about an experimental drug therapy for muscular
   dystrophy by announcing that patients in the trial
   failed to reach the milestone for improvement
   that the company had set in its protocol.

5. Low Doses of Ataluren Did Improve
   Muscular Dystrophy Symptoms   87

   John Gever

   A physician associated with muscular dystrophy
   drug research says that a trial for the drug
   ataluren should have been considered a success.
   Even though patients did not achieve the preset
   milestone, many came close, showing that the
   drug is effective but that the manufacturer may
   have set too-high a benchmark.

6. White Muscular Dystrophy Patients Live
   Longer than Blacks with MD   91
   Madison Park

   A study finds a steep disparity in length of
   life between white and black Americans who
   develop muscular dystrophy. The average
   difference is ten to twelve years.

CHAPTER 3 **Personal Narratives**

1. A Woman with a Rare Form of Muscular
   Dystrophy Talks About Living with
   the Disease   96
   Mandy Van Benthuysen

   Limb-girdle muscular dystrophy, a relatively
   rare form of MD, struck the author when she
   was four years old. Now an adult, she speaks
   out on living and thriving, despite the disease.

2. An American Muscular Dystrophy Patient
   Goes to China for Stem Cell Treatment   99
   Russ Kleve

   A man suffering from facioscapulohumeral
   muscular dystrophy records his experience of
   traveling to China to get stem cell treatment for
   his disease and the results after several months.

3. Life Without a Smile   107
   Sarabjit Parmar

   A young woman describes a socially debilitating
   aspect of her muscular dystrophy and how she
   has learned to live with it.

   Glossary   111
   Chronology   114
   Organizations to Contact   116
   For Further Reading   120
   Index   123

FOREWORD

"Medicine, to produce health, has to examine disease."
—Plutarch

Independent research on a health issue is often the first step to complement discussions with a physician. But locating accurate, well-organized, understandable medical information can be a challenge. A simple Internet search on terms such as "cancer" or "diabetes," for example, returns an intimidating number of results. Sifting through the results can be daunting, particularly when some of the information is inconsistent or even contradictory. The Greenhaven Press series Perspectives on Diseases and Disorders offers a solution to the often overwhelming nature of researching diseases and disorders.

From the clinical to the personal, titles in the Perspectives on Diseases and Disorders series provide students and other researchers with authoritative, accessible information in unique anthologies that include basic information about the disease or disorder, controversial aspects of diagnosis and treatment, and first-person accounts of those impacted by the disease. The result is a well-rounded combination of primary and secondary sources that, together, provide the reader with a better understanding of the disease or disorder.

Each volume in Perspectives on Diseases and Disorders explores a particular disease or disorder in detail. Material for each volume is carefully selected from a wide range of sources, including encyclopedias, journals, newspapers, nonfiction books, speeches, government documents, pamphlets, organization newsletters, and position papers. Articles in the first chapter provide an authoritative, up-to-date overview that covers symptoms, causes and effects, treatments, cures, and medical advances. The second chapter presents a substantial number of opposing viewpoints on controversial treatments and other current debates relating to the volume topic. The third chapter offers a variety of personal perspectives on the disease or disorder. Patients, doctors, caregivers, and loved ones represent just some of the voices found in this narrative chapter.

Each Perspectives on Diseases and Disorders volume also includes:

- An **annotated table of contents** that provides a brief summary of each article in the volume.
- An **introduction** specific to the volume topic.
- Full-color **charts and graphs** to illustrate key points, concepts, and theories.
- Full-color **photos** that show aspects of the disease or disorder and enhance textual material.
- **"Fast Facts"** that highlight pertinent additional statistics and surprising points.
- A **glossary** providing users with definitions of important terms.
- A **chronology** of important dates relating to the disease or disorder.
- An annotated list of **organizations to contact** for students and other readers seeking additional information.
- A **bibliography** of additional books and periodicals for further research.
- A detailed **subject index** that allows readers to quickly find the information they need.

Whether a student researching a disorder, a patient recently diagnosed with a disease, or an individual who simply wants to learn more about a particular disease or disorder, a reader who turns to Perspectives on Diseases and Disorders will find a wealth of information in each volume that offers not only basic information, but also vigorous debate from multiple perspectives.

INTRODUCTION

Muscular dystrophy is a tragic genetic error over which some brave people triumph. Muscular dystrophy, or MD for short, is not just a single disease. It is rather a group of related genetic disorders characterized by progressive and often fatal weakening of the muscles.

Their cause is not a bacterium or virus but an erroneous code in a gene. That error prevents a victim's body from producing a protein called dystrophin that is crucial to the health of muscle cells. There is no cure for muscular dystrophy and no effective treatment. And yet, many heroic people with MD manage to lead meaningful and productive lives.

One such person is a young Canadian woman who, online, calls herself "JadeLabG." At twenty years old, she has coped with MD since the age of four. Despite long experience with muscular dystrophy, she refuses to let it dominate her life. "Now I will admit," she writes in her blog for *The Experience Project* on November 9, 2007, "it has a HUGE Influence Over My Life. But I have always tried to do as much as I can, despite my disability. To many people, including my past pediatricians, MD has been a death sentence. I was 4 years old when I was 'diagnosed' with MD. My parents were told I would not live much past the age of 9. Well here I am, 11 years later! I'm still here, fighting along and trying to have a laugh."

And not just a laugh. She also plays the flute, sings, and has built meaningful relationships with others— especially her fiancé. JadeLabG offers insight into the secret of her success: attitude. "There are a number of things that have helped me get this far in my life," she writes. "The first & most important thing is a positive attitude. . . . Life is too short. Make the most of today, be kind to others, & keep smiling."

Of course, it helps to be lucky. JadeLabG was lucky to beat the odds and live into her third decade, lucky to have a warm and supportive family around her, and lucky to live in a country that provides comprehensive health care to someone such as herself.

Not everyone shares her good fortune. Boys born with Duchenne muscular dystrophy—the most common kind of MD—often succumb in their teens. Children with MD are often shunned by others, even though their condition is not contagious. The cost of care can be an enormous burden on families, especially in the later stages when everything from wheelchairs to respirators to full-time caregivers may be required.

In all, there are nine main varieties of muscular dystrophy and hundreds of other genetic diseases that have partial MD symptoms. The most common forms, Duchenne and Becker MD, mainly afflict boys and men. But women experience their share of muscular dystrophy as well, in varieties such as limb-girdle MD.

What all MD has in common is this: a genetic mutation that causes malformation of the protein dystrophin. Without dystrophin, the internal framework of a muscle cell collapses, like a tent with faulty poles. This sets off a cascade of troubles leading to the eventual death of the cell. As muscle cells die off, they are replaced by fat cells or connective tissue.

The most common forms of muscular dystrophy are sex-linked. That is to say, the mutation that causes the disease appears in the chromosomes that determine sex. The X chromosome is female, and the Y chromosome is male. (They are so called because of their shapes, which resemble the letters.) Each egg contains an X chromosome; each sperm contains either an X or a Y. Two Xs mean a girl; an X and a Y result in a boy.

But there is an unfortunate catch for boys. The Y chromosome is tiny. It has barely enough genes to get the job of sex-determination done. The X chromosome, by comparison, has vastly more genes. Two Xs will match up genes across the board, and whichever one carries the best versions will generally prevail. This affords girls a measure of protection against sex-linked genetic diseases. However, when a Y chromosome meets up with an X that contains a defective dystrophin-producing gene, it has no alternative to offer. Duchenne muscular dystrophy is by far the most common form, afflicting about one in four thousand boys. As described above, it is a sex-linked recessive disorder. When an X chromosome carrying the Duchenne mutation meets a healthy X chromosome, the healthy chromosome dominates.

That is why a woman may carry the gene that causes muscular dystrophy but suffer no effects. If she has a daughter, the chances are very high that the girl will not have the disease (her father would also have to carry the defective X for it to occur). If this woman gives birth to a boy, however, there is a strong chance that he will come down with the disease, since his father's Y chromosome cannot protect him.

Of course, none of this was known in the nineteenth century, when Guillaume Duchenne de Boulogne turned his attention to a mysterious condition afflicting boys in his native France. Despite his rather grandiose name, Duchenne had been born into humble circumstances. He was the son of fishermen, the only one in his family to attend college. He went on to study medicine and graduated as a physician from an academy in Paris in 1831.

He might have merely practiced, but his intense curiosity led him to perform research into muscles. At first, he experimented by placing electrodes under the skin of patients and then forcing their muscles to contract by running a current through them. This painful procedure eventually gave way to more humane methods, but in the

In 1856 French physician Guillaume Duchenne de Boulogne (left) experimented on muscles by placing electrodes under the skin of patients and then forcing their muscles to contract by running an electric current through them. He described the failure of muscles that is characteristic of muscular dystrophy. (© Hulton Archive/Getty Images)

meantime Duchenne accumulated a wealth of insights into the operation of the human muscle system. He was therefore well prepared to describe in detail the gradual failure of muscles that is characteristic of muscular dystrophy. He began doing so in a series of monographs published in the early 1860s.

Although unable to explain its origins or recommend any curative treatment, Duchenne received credit for the discovery of the disease. This was not entirely just, as at least two other researchers, beginning with the Italian medical professor Gaetano Conte, had also detected the disease decades earlier. Nevertheless, Duchenne's name came to be associated with the most widespread version of muscular dystrophy.

At about the same time that Duchenne was publishing research into muscular dystrophy, an obscure monk named Gregor Mendel was conducting experiments in his garden in central Europe. By carefully cross-breeding peas and recording the results, Mendel was able to infer the method by which genes carry traits into a new generation. His research failed to circulate widely until the twentieth century, and so the genetic basis of muscular dystrophy would remain unknown until long after Duchenne's death in 1875.

Even after the general basis of the disease was understood, little could be done to treat it. Discovery of the actual gene responsible for Duchenne muscular dystrophy would not come about until 1987.

At that time, there was much hope in the air that gene therapy would soon transform medicine and lead to cures for genetic diseases such as muscular dystrophy. But hope turned to disappointment as gene therapy turned out to be fraught with difficulties. Finding a safe means of delivering genes proved a major obstacle. One healthy volunteer died after the viruses carrying genes into his body provoked a massive overreaction of his immune system.

The first human trial of gene therapy for muscular dystrophy did not take place for two decades after the discovery of the disease-causing gene. In 2010 the Muscular Dystrophy Association announced that researchers had produced a modest success in the trial. By injecting viruses carrying healthy muscle genes into limb-girdle muscular dystrophy patients, they succeeded in coaxing cells in the patients' bodies into producing dystrophin for up to six months.

Such a result hardly amounts to a cure. But for the first time, it is possible to say that the long-elusive cure is in sight. If medical researchers can build on their progress to date, it may well be that in the future, those born with muscular dystrophy will be able to live long and healthy lives.

CHAPTER 1

Understanding Muscular Dystrophy

An Overview of Muscular Dystrophy

Nada Quercia

Muscular dystrophy (MD) is a complex of related genetic diseases. In the following selection Nada Quercia defines and describes the disease and its underpinnings, as well as its symptoms, treatments, and varieties. Certain forms of muscular dystrophy require that a person inherit copies of the faulty genes from both parents, but for other types a single gene is sufficient, she explains. Yet other cases arise from spontaneous mutations in the fertilized egg. Many of the MD genes are sex-linked, with the result that the disease is more common in men than in women. It manifests in many different forms, but what these forms have in common is a wasting of muscle tissue that refuses to respond to treatment. Quercia is a genetic counselor in the Division of Clinical and Metabolic Genetics at the Hospital for Sick Children in Toronto, Canada.

Photo on facing page. In this ancient Egyptian relief from 1480 BC, the figure shown is suffering from muscular dystrophy. The Egyptian queen Hatshepsut is the earliest known person who may have had the disease. (© **Science Source/Photo Researchers, Inc.**)

Muscular dystrophy [MD] is the name for a group of inherited disorders in which strength and muscle bulk gradually decline. Nine types of muscular dystrophies are generally recognized. . . .

Muscular dystrophies are genetic conditions, meaning they are caused by alterations in genes. Genes, which are linked together on chromosomes, have two functions; they code for the production of proteins, and they are the material of inheritance. Parents pass along genes to their children, providing them with a complete set of instructions for making their own proteins.

Because both parents contribute genetic material to their offspring, each child carries two copies of almost every gene, one from each parent. For some conditions to occur, both copies must be altered. Such conditions are called autosomal recessive conditions. . . . A person with only one altered copy, called a carrier, will not have the condition, but may pass the altered gene on to his [or her] children. When two carriers have children, the chances of having a child with the condition is one in four for each pregnancy.

Other conditions occur when only one altered gene copy is present. . . . When a person affected by the condition has a child with someone not affected, the chances of having an affected child is one in two.

Sex Differences

Because of chromosomal differences between the sexes, some genes are not present in two copies. The chromosomes that determine whether a person is male or female are called the X and Y chromosomes. A person with two X chromosomes is female, while a person with one X and one Y is male. While the X chromosome carries many genes, the Y chromosome carries almost none. Therefore, a male has only one copy of each gene on the X chromosome, and if it is altered, he will have the condition that alteration causes. Such conditions are said to

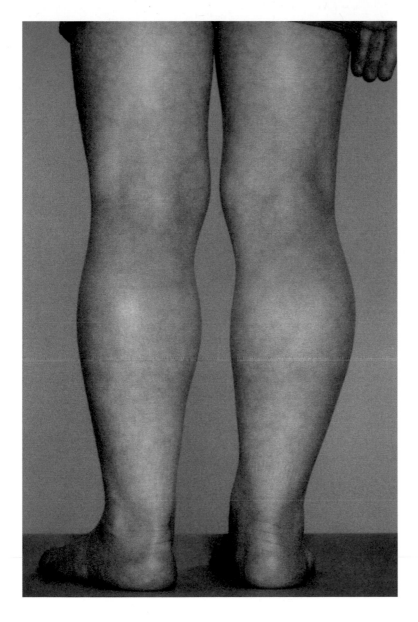

Duchenne muscular dystrophy is a genectic disorder characterized by the wasting away of muscle and the loss of muscle function. A characteristic symptom is the replacement of muscle by fat. (© **Biophoto Associates/ Photo Researchers, Inc.**)

be X-linked. . . . Women are not usually affected by X-linked conditions, since they will likely have one unaltered copy between the two chromosomes. Some female carriers of DMD [Duchenne muscular dystrophy] have a mild form of the condition, probably because their one unaltered gene copy is shut down in some of their cells.

Women carriers of X-linked conditions have a one in two chance of passing the altered gene on to each child born. Daughters who inherit the altered gene will be carriers. A son born without the altered gene will be free of the condition and cannot pass it on to his children. A son born with the altered gene will have the condition. He will pass the altered gene on to each of his daughters, who will then be [only] carriers, but to none of his sons (because they inherit his Y chromosome).

Not all genetic alterations are inherited. As many as one third of the cases of DMD are due to new mutations that arise during egg formation in the mother. New mutations are less common in other forms of muscular dystrophy. . . .

Symptoms of Various Dystrophy Types

All of the muscular dystrophies are marked by muscle weakness as the major symptom. The distribution of symptoms, age of onset, and progression differ significantly. Pain is sometimes a symptom of each, usually due to the effects of weakness on joint position.

Duchenne Muscular Dystrophy (DMD). A boy with Duchenne muscular dystrophy usually begins to show symptoms as a pre-schooler. The legs are affected first, making walking difficult and causing balance problems. Most patients walk three to six months later than expected and have difficulty running. Later on, a boy with DMD will push his hands against his knees to rise to a standing position, to compensate for leg weakness. About the same time, his calves will begin to enlarge, though with fibrous tissue rather than with muscle, and feel firm and rubbery; this condition gives DMD one of its alternate names, pseudohypertrophic muscular dystrophy. He will widen his stance to maintain balance, and walk with a waddling gait to advance his weakened legs. Contractures (permanent muscle tightening) usually begin by age five or six, most severely in the calf muscles. This pulls the foot down and back, forcing the boy to walk on tip-toes, and further decreases balance. Climbing stairs and rising unaided may become impossible by age nine or ten, and most boys use a wheelchair for mobility by the age of 12. Weakening of the trunk muscles around this age often leads to scoliosis (a side-to-side spine curvature) and kyphosis (a front-to-back curvature).

The most serious weakness of DMD is weakness of the diaphragm, the sheet of muscles at the top of the abdomen that perform the main work of breathing and coughing. Diaphragm weakness leads to reduced energy and stamina, and increased lung infection because of the inability to cough effectively. Young men with DMD often live into their twenties and beyond, provided they

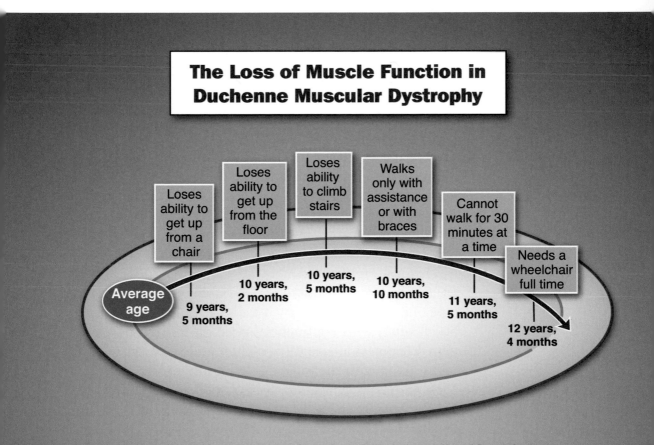

The Loss of Muscle Function in Duchenne Muscular Dystrophy

Loses ability to get up from a chair — Average age — 9 years, 5 months

Loses ability to get up from the floor — 10 years, 2 months

Loses ability to climb stairs — 10 years, 5 months

Walks only with assistance or with braces — 10 years, 10 months

Cannot walk for 30 minutes at a time — 11 years, 5 months

Needs a wheelchair full time — 12 years, 4 months

Taken from: Muscular Dystrophy Association, *Getting the Diagnosis, Journey of Love: A Parent's Guide to Duchenne Muscular Dystrophy.* Tucson, AZ: MDA, 1999. mww.mdausa.org.

have mechanical ventilation assistance and good respiratory hygiene.

Among males with DMD, the incidence of cardiomyopathy (weakness of the heart muscle), increases steadily in teenage years. Almost all patients have cardiomyopathy after 18 years of age. It has also been shown that carrier females are at increased risk for cardiomyopathy and should also be screened.

About one third of males with DMD experience specific learning disabilities, including difficulty learning by ear rather than by sight and difficulty paying attention to long lists of instructions. Individualized educational programs usually compensate well for these disabilities.

Becker Muscular Dystrophy (BMD). The symptoms of BMD usually appear in late childhood to early adulthood. Though the progression of symptoms may parallel that of DMD, the symptoms are usually milder and the course more variable. The same pattern of leg weakness, unsteadiness, and contractures occur later for the young man with BMD, often allowing independent walking into the twenties or early thirties. Scoliosis may occur, but is usually milder and progresses more slowly. Cardiomyopathy occurs more commonly in BMD. Problems may include irregular heartbeats (arrhythmias) and congestive heart failure. Symptoms may include fatigue, shortness of breath, chest pain, and dizziness. Respiratory weakness also occurs, and may lead to the need for mechanical ventilation.

Emery-Dreifuss Muscular Dystrophy (EDMD). This type of muscular dystrophy usually begins in early childhood, often with contractures preceding muscle weakness. Weakness affects the shoulder and upper arm initially, along with the calf muscles, leading to foot-drop. Most men with EDMD survive into middle age, although an abnormality in the heart's rhythm (heart block) may be fatal if not treated with a pacemaker.

Limb-Girdle Muscular Dystrophy (LGMD). While there are several genes that cause the various types of LGMD, two major clinical forms of LGMD are usually recognized. A severe childhood form is similar in appearance to DMD, but is inherited as an autosomal recessive trait. Symptoms of adult-onset LGMD usually appear in a person's teens or twenties, and are marked by progressive weakness and wasting of the muscles closest to the trunk. Contractures may occur, and the ability to walk is usually lost about 20 years after onset. Some people with LGMD develop respiratory weakness that requires use of a ventilator. Life-span may be somewhat shortened. Autosomal dominant forms usually occur later in life and progress relatively slowly.

Facioscapulohumeral Muscular Dystrophy (FSH). FSH varies in its severity and age of onset, even among members of the same family. Symptoms most commonly begin in the teens or early twenties, though infant or childhood onset is possible. Symptoms tend to be more severe in those with earlier onset. The condition is named for the regions of the body most severely affected by the condition: muscles of the face (facio-), shoulders (scapulo-), and upper arms (humeral). Hips and legs may be affected as well. Children with FSH may develop partial or complete deafness.

The first symptom noticed is often difficulty lifting objects above the shoulders. The weakness may be greater on one side than the other. Shoulder weakness also causes the shoulder blades to jut backward, called scapular winging. Muscles in the upper arm often lose bulk sooner than those of the forearm, giving a "Popeye" [cartoon character] appearance to the arms. Facial weakness may lead to loss of facial expression, difficulty closing the eyes completely, and inability to drink through a straw, blow up a balloon, or whistle. A person with FSH may not be able to wrinkle [his or her] forehead. Contracture of the calf muscles may cause foot-drop, leading to frequent tripping over curbs or rough spots. People with earlier onset often require a wheelchair for mobility, while those with later onset rarely do.

Myotonic Dystrophy. Symptoms of myotonic dystrophy include facial weakness and a slack jaw, drooping eyelids (ptosis), and muscle wasting in the forearms and calves. A person with myotonic dystrophy has difficulty relaxing his grasp, especially if the object is cold. Myotonic dystrophy affects heart muscle, causing arrhythmias and heart block, and the muscles of the digestive system, leading to motility disorders and constipation. Other body systems are affected as well; myotonic dystrophy may cause cataracts, retinal degeneration, mental deficiency, frontal balding, skin disorders, testicular atrophy, sleep apnea, and insulin resistance. An increased need or desire for sleep is common, as is diminished motivation. The condition is extremely variable; some individuals show profound weakness as a newborn (congenital myotonic dystrophy), others show mental retardation in childhood, many show characteristic facial features and muscle wasting in adulthood, while the most mildly affected individuals show only cataracts in middle age with no other symptoms. Individuals with a severe form of myotonic dystrophy typically have severe disabilities within 20 years of onset, although most do not require a wheelchair even late in life.

Oculopharyngeal Muscular Dystrophy (OPMD). OPMD usually begins in a person's thirties or forties, with weakness in the muscles controlling the eyes and throat. Symptoms include drooping eyelids and difficulty swallowing (dysphagia). Weakness progresses to other muscles of the face, neck, and occasionally the upper limbs. Swallowing difficulty may cause aspiration, or the introduction of food or saliva into the airways. Pneumonia may follow.

FAST FACT

The life expectancy of muscular dystrophy patients varies widely, depending on the form of the disease and the condition of the individual, but, in general, MD cuts life short.

Distal Muscular Dystrophy (DD). DD usually begins in the twenties or thirties, with weakness in the hands, forearms, and lower legs. Difficulty with fine movements such as typing or fastening buttons may be the first symptoms. Symptoms progress slowly, and the condition usually does not affect life span.

Congenital Muscular Dystrophy (CMD). CMD is marked by severe muscle weakness from birth, with infants displaying "floppiness," very poor muscle tone, and they often have trouble moving their limbs or head against gravity. Mental function is normal but some are never able to walk. They may live into young adulthood or beyond. In contrast, children with Fukuyama CMD are rarely able to walk, and have severe mental retardation. Most children with this type of CMD die in childhood.

The Diagnosis of Muscular Dystrophy

The diagnosis of muscular dystrophy involves a careful medical history and a thorough physical exam to determine the distribution of symptoms and to rule out other causes. Family history may give important clues, since all the muscular dystrophies are genetic conditions (though no family history will be evident in the event of new mutations; in autosomal recessive inheritance, the family history may also be negative).

Lab tests may include:

- Blood level of the muscle enzyme creatine kinase (CK). CK levels rise in the blood due to muscle damage, and may be seen in some conditions even before symptoms appear.
- Muscle biopsy, in which a small piece of muscle tissue is removed for microscopic examination. Changes in the structure of muscle cells and presence of fibrous tissue or other aberrant structures are characteristic of different forms of muscular dystrophy. The muscle tissue can also be stained

to detect the presence or absence of particular proteins, including dystrophin.

- Electromyogram (EMG). This electrical test is used to examine the response of the muscles to stimulation. Decreased response is seen in muscular dystrophy. Other characteristic changes are seen in DM [dermatomyositis].
- Genetic tests. Several of the muscular dystrophies can be positively identified by testing for the presence of the altered gene involved. Accurate genetic tests are available for DMD, BMD, DM, several forms of LGMD, and EDMD. Genetic testing for some of these conditions in future pregnancies of an affected individual or parents of an affected individual can be done before birth through amniocentesis or chorionic villus sampling. Prenatal testing can only be undertaken after the diagnosis in the affected individual has been genetically confirmed and the couple has been counseled regarding the risks of recurrence.
- Other specific tests as necessary. For EDMD, DMD and BMD, for example, an electrocardiogram may be needed to test heart function, and hearing tests are performed for children with FSH.

For most forms of muscular dystrophy, accurate diagnosis is not difficult when done by someone familiar with the range of conditions. There are exceptions, however. Even with a muscle biopsy, it may be difficult to distinguish between FSH and another muscle condition, polymyositis. Childhood-onset LGMD is often mistaken for the much more common DMD, especially when it occurs in boys. BMD with an early onset appears very similar to DMD, and a genetic test may be needed to accurately distinguish them. The muscular dystrophies may be confused with conditions involving the motor neurons, such as spinal muscular atrophy; conditions of the neuromuscular junction, such as myasthenia gravis;

and other muscle conditions, as all involve generalized weakness of varying distribution.

Prenatal diagnosis (testing of the baby while in the womb) can be done for those types of muscular dystrophy where the specific disease-causing gene alteration has been identified in a previously affected family member. Prenatal diagnosis can be done utilizing DNA extracted from tissue obtained by chorionic villus sampling or amniocentesis.

Medical Treatments

Drugs. There are no cures for any of the muscular dystrophies. Prednisone, a corticosteroid, has been shown to delay the progression of DMD somewhat, for reasons that are still unclear. Some have reported improvement in strength and function in patients treated with a single dose. Improvement begins within ten days and plateaus after three months. Long-term benefit has not been demonstrated. Prednisone is also prescribed for BMD, though no controlled studies have tested its benefit. A study is under way in the use of gentamicin, an antibiotic that may slow down the symptoms of DMD in a small number of cases. No other drugs are currently known to have an effect on the course of any other muscular dystrophy.

Treatment of muscular dystrophy is mainly directed at preventing the complications of weakness, including decreased mobility and dexterity, contractures, scoliosis, heart alterations, and respiratory insufficiency.

Physical therapy. Physical therapy, regular stretching in particular, is used to maintain the range of motion of affected muscles and to prevent or delay contractures. Braces are used as well, especially on the ankles and feet to prevent tip-toeing. Full-leg braces may be used in children with DMD to prolong the period of independent walking. Strengthening other muscle groups to compensate for weakness may be possible if the affected muscles are few and isolated, as in the earlier stages of the milder muscular dystrophies. Regular, nonstrenuous exercise helps maintain general good health. Strenuous exercise is usually not recommended, since it may damage muscles further.

Surgery. When contractures become more pronounced, tenotomy surgery may be performed. In this operation, the tendon of the contractured muscle is cut, and the limb is braced in its normal resting position while the tendon regrows. In FSH, surgical fixation of the scapula can help compensate for shoulder weakness. For a person with OPMD, surgical lifting of the eyelids may help compensate for weakened muscular control. For a person with DM, sleep apnea may be treated surgically to maintain an open airway. Scoliosis surgery is often needed in boys with DMD, but much less often in other muscular dystrophies. Surgery is recommended at a much lower degree of curvature for DMD than for scoliosis due to other conditions, since the decline in respiratory function in DMD makes surgery at a later time dangerous. In this surgery, the vertebrae are fused together to maintain the spine in the upright position. Steel rods are inserted at the time of operation to keep the spine rigid while the bones grow together.

When any type of surgery is performed in patients with muscular dystrophy, anesthesia must be carefully selected. People with MD are susceptible to a severe reaction, known as malignant hyperthermia, when given halothane anesthetic.

Occupational therapy. The occupational therapist suggests techniques and tools to compensate for the loss of strength and dexterity. Strategies may include modifications in the home, adaptive utensils and dressing aids, compensatory movements and positioning, wheelchair accessories, or communication aids.

Nutrition. Good nutrition helps to promote general health in all the muscular dystrophies. No special diet or supplement has been shown to be of use in any of the conditions. The weakness in the throat muscles seen especially in OPMD and later DMD may necessitate the use of a gastrostomy tube inserted in the stomach to provide nutrition directly.

Cardiac care. The arrhythmias of EDMD and BMD may be treatable with antiarrhythmia drugs. A pacemaker may be implanted if these do not provide adequate control. Heart transplants are increasingly common for men with BMD. A complete cardiac evaluation is recommended at least once in all carrier females of DMD and EDMD.

Respiratory care. People who develop weakness of the diaphragm or other ventilatory muscles may require a mechanical ventilator to continue breathing deeply enough. Air may be administered through a nasal mask or mouthpiece, or through a tracheostomy tube, which is inserted through a surgical incision through the neck and into the windpipe. Most people with muscular dystrophy do not need a tracheostomy, although some may prefer it to continual use of a mask or mouthpiece. Supplemental oxygen is not needed. Good hygiene of the lungs is critical for health and long-term survival of a person with weakened ventilatory muscles. Assisted cough techniques provide the strength needed to clear the airways of secretions; an assisted cough machine is also available and provides excellent results.

Experimental treatments. Two experimental procedures aiming to cure DMD have attracted a great deal of attention in the past decade. In myoblast transfer, millions of immature muscle cells are injected into an affected muscle. The goal of the treatment is to promote the growth of the injected cells, replacing the abnormal host cells with healthy new ones. Myoblast transfer is under investigation but remains experimental.

Gene therapy introduces unaltered copies of the altered gene into muscle cells. The goal is to allow the existing muscle cells to use the new gene to produce the protein it cannot make with its abnormal gene. Problems with gene therapy research have included immune rejection of the virus used to introduce the gene, loss of gene function after several weeks, and an inability to get the gene to enough cells to make a functional difference in the affected muscle. . . .

Genetic counseling. Individuals with muscular dystrophy and their families may benefit from genetic counseling for information on the condition and recurrence risks for future pregnancies.

Prognosis and Prevention

The expected life span for a male with DMD has increased significantly in the past two decades. Most young men will live into their early or mid-twenties. Respiratory infections become an increasing problem as their breathing becomes weaker, and these infections are usually the cause of death.

The course of the other muscular dystrophies is more variable; expected life spans and degrees of disability are hard to predict, but may be related to age of onset and initial symptoms. Prediction is made more difficult because, as new genes are discovered, it is becoming clear that several of the dystrophies are not uniform disorders, but rather symptom groups caused by different genes.

People with dystrophies with significant heart involvement (BMD, EDMD, myotonic dystrophy) may nonetheless have almost normal life spans, provided that cardiac complications are monitored and treated aggressively. The respiratory involvement of BMD and LGMD similarly require careful and prompt treatment.

There is no way to prevent any of the muscular dystrophies in a person who has the genes responsible for these disorders. Accurate genetic tests, including prenatal tests, are available for some of the muscular dystrophies. Results of these tests may be useful for purposes of family planning.

National Programs Aim to Understand and Treat Muscular Dystrophy

National Institutes of Health

After Congress passed an act to support research into muscular dystrophy, the US Department of Health and Human Services (HHS) was tasked with reporting annually on related progress. In the following selection excerpts from the 2007 report of the National Institutes of Health (NIH), a division of HHS, are presented. The NIH outlines its efforts to uncover the causes of muscular dystrophy and discover effective treatments. Its various experimental trials are described, along with projects to improve the screening of potential sufferers and the training of researchers and physicians who may encounter muscular dystrophy. The National Institutes of Health serves as the nation's premier medical research agency.

In December 2001, President George W. Bush signed into law the Muscular Dystrophy Community Assistance, Research and Education Amendments of 2001 (the MD-CARE Act, Public Law 107-84). . . .

SOURCE: National Institutes of Health, Department of Health and Human Services, "Report to Congress on Implementation of the MD-CARE Amendments of 2001," July 2007.

This report is presented as an annual report to Congress on the implementation of the Act. This is the fifth annual report, which highlights recent activities at NIH [National Institutes of Health] and CDC [Centers for Disease Control and Prevention] to advance our understanding and treatment of the muscular dystrophies. . . .

The muscular dystrophies are a group of diseases that cause weakness and progressive degeneration of skeletal muscles. There are many different forms of muscular dystrophy, which differ in their mode of inheritance, age of onset, severity, and pattern of muscles affected. Most types of muscular dystrophy are, in fact, multisystem disorders with manifestations in body systems including the heart, gastrointestinal and nervous systems, endocrine glands, skin, eyes, and other organs.

Types and Subtypes of Muscular Dystrophy

Duchenne muscular dystrophy (DMD) is the most common childhood form of muscular dystrophy. DMD usually becomes clinically evident when a child begins walking. Patients typically require a wheelchair by age 10 to 12 and die in their late teens or early 20s. More than 15 years ago, researchers supported by the NIH and the Muscular Dystrophy Association (MDA) identified the gene for the protein dystrophin which, when absent, causes DMD. The dystrophin gene is the largest known gene in humans. Since the gene is on the X-chromosome, this disorder affects primarily males. Females who are carriers have milder symptoms. Sporadic mutations in this gene occur frequently, accounting for a third of cases. The remaining two-thirds of cases are inherited in a recessive pattern. Becker muscular dystrophy (BMD) is a less severe variant of the disease and is caused by the production of a truncated but partially functional form of dystrophin. Dystrophin is part of a complex structure involving several other protein components. The "dystrophin-glycoprotein

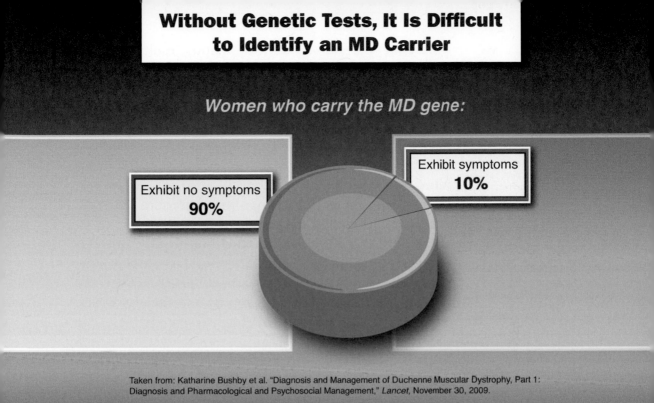

Without Genetic Tests, It Is Difficult to Identify an MD Carrier

Women who carry the MD gene:

Exhibit no symptoms
90%

Exhibit symptoms
10%

Taken from: Katharine Bushby et al. "Diagnosis and Management of Duchenne Muscular Dystrophy, Part 1: Diagnosis and Pharmacological and Psychosocial Management," *Lancet*, November 30, 2009.

complex" helps anchor the structural skeleton within the muscle cells, through the outer membrane of each cell, to the tissue framework that surrounds each cell. Due to defects in this assembly, muscle contraction leads to disruption of the outer membrane of the muscle cells and eventual weakening and wasting of the muscle.

Myotonic dystrophy is the most common adult form of muscular dystrophy. It is marked by myotonia (an inability to relax muscles following contraction) as well as muscle wasting and weakness. Myotonic dystrophy varies in severity and manifestations and affects many body systems in addition to skeletal muscles, including the heart, endocrine organs, eyes, and gastrointestinal tract. Myotonic dystrophy follows an autosomal dominant pattern of inheritance. This means that the disorder can occur in either sex when a person inherits a single defective gene from either parent. Myotonic dystrophy results from the expansion of a short repeat in the DNA sequence (CTG in one gene or CCTG in another gene). More simply put, the inherited gene defect is an abnormally long repetition of a three- or four-letter "word" in the genetic code— normally, this "word" is repeated a number of times, but in people with myotonic dystrophy, it is repeated many more times. While the exact mechanism of action is not known, this molecular change may interfere with the production of important muscle proteins.

Facioscapulohumeral muscular dystrophy (FSHD) initially affects muscles of the face (facio), shoulders (scapulo), and upper arms (humeral) with progressive weakness. Symptoms usually develop in the teenage years. Some affected individuals become severely disabled. The pattern of inheritance is, like myotonic dystrophy, autosomal dominant, but the underlying genetic defect is poorly understood. Most cases are associated with a deletion near the end of chromosome.

The limb-girdle muscular dystrophies (LGMDs) all show a similar distribution of muscle weakness, affecting both upper arms and legs. Many forms of LGMD have been identified, showing different patterns of inheritance (autosomal recessive vs. autosomal dominant). In an autosomal recessive pattern of inheritance, an individual receives two copies of the defective gene, one from each parent. The recessive LGMDs are more frequent than the dominant forms, and usually have childhood or teenage onset. The dominant LGMDs usually show adult onset. Some of the recessive forms have been associated with defects in proteins that make up the dystrophin-glycoprotein complex.

The congenital muscular dystrophies, another class of muscular dystrophies, also include several disorders with a range of symptoms. Muscle degeneration may be mild or severe. Problems may be restricted to skeletal muscle, or muscle degeneration may be paired with effects on the brain and other organ systems. A number of the forms of the congenital muscular dystrophies are caused by defects in proteins that are thought to have some relationship to the dystrophin-glycoprotein complex and to the connections between muscle cells and their surrounding cellular structure. Some forms of congenital muscular dystrophy show severe brain malformations, such as lissencephaly (a "smooth" appearance to the brain due to the absence of normal convolutions—or folds—in the brain) and hydrocephalus (an excessive accumulation of fluid in the brain).

Several other forms of muscular dystrophy also occur. Oculopharyngeal muscular dystrophy, which causes weakness in the eye, throat, and facial muscles, followed by pelvic and shoulder muscle weakness, has been attributed to a short repeat expansion in a gene which regulates the translation of the genetic code into functional

Congenital muscular dystrophies include several disorders with a range of symptoms. They include muscle degeneration, which can be mild to severe and which may be paired with effects on the brain and other organ systems. (© Medical-on-Line/Alamy)

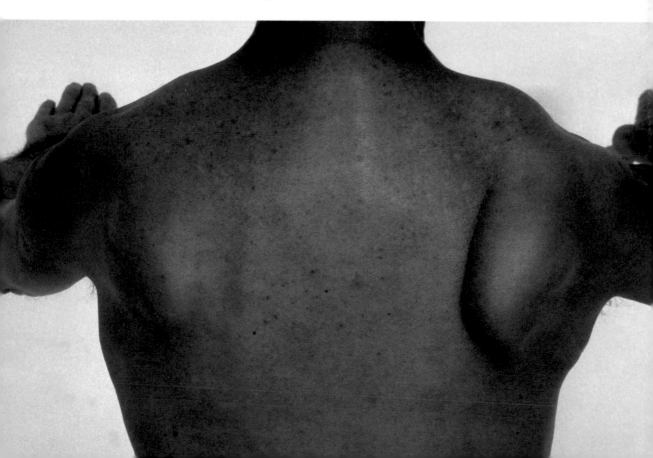

proteins. Emery-Dreifuss muscular dystrophy is characterized by weakness in the shoulder girdle and lower legs, as well as the development of contractures (tightening or loss of motion) in regions of the body, particularly the elbows, Achilles tendons, and neck. Defects in proteins that make up the cell's nucleus are implicated in the disorder. Miyoshi myopathy, one of the distal muscular dystrophies, causes initial weakness in the calf muscles, and is caused by defects in the same gene responsible for one form of LGMD, suggesting that progress against one form of muscular dystrophy may lead to a better understanding of other forms as well.

Treatments and Responses

Currently, no treatment can stop or reverse the progression of any form of muscular dystrophy. Symptomatic treatments such as physical therapy, use of appliances for support, corrective orthopedic surgery and drugs may improve the quality of life for some individuals. However, even though some drugs such as steroids can slow the progression of DMD, there are side effects. Several therapeutic approaches, including gene therapy, cell-based strategies, and strategies to inhibit muscle degeneration have shown promise in cell-based systems and in animal models and some early clinical trials in humans have begun. Examples of these approaches include the use of drugs to reduce muscle membrane damage, cell-based replacement therapies, functional compensation for dystrophin by upregulation of certain proteins, increasing muscle mass via inhibition of other proteins that negatively regulate muscle growth, inhibiting muscle protein degradation, and strategies to bypass the mutations that cause disease.

The following provides an overview of the program activities of the main NIH components currently supporting muscular dystrophy research. Although the intent of each section is to summarize the contributions of each individual Institute, it is important to recognize that many of these are collaborative activities. The NIH Institutes and Centers involved in muscular dystrophy are committed to working together to identify and support new initiatives to expand the NIH muscular dystrophy portfolio. NIH anticipates that a collaborative, multifaceted approach will yield the most significant advances in understanding and treating the muscular dystrophies.

National Institute of Neurological Disorders and Stroke (NINDS). NINDS supports intramural and extramural research on many forms of muscular dystrophy ranging from basic studies of normal protein function through projects on gene, stem cell, and drug therapies at levels from the development of experimental therapeutics through clinical trials. The NINDS also continues to support a very active portfolio of basic research on the neuromuscular junction, the terminal between a nerve cell and muscle fiber. Much of this basic research is critical to advancing our understanding of the mechanisms underlying the muscular dystrophies. In 1987, researchers supported by NINDS and the Muscular Dystrophy Association discovered that dystrophin mutations cause DMD and BMD. NINDS has continued to support subsequent work on understanding the role and function of the dystrophin-glycoprotein complex both in normal muscle and in muscular dystrophy-affected muscle tissue. The NINDS funds research relevant to understanding the molecular and genetic basis of FSHD, as well as research relevant to myotonic dystrophy, LGMD, and other forms of muscular dystrophy and neuromuscular disorders. Another area of focus is the improved diagnosis of the muscular dystrophies. For example, NINDS supports the United Dystrophinopathy Project at the University of Utah, which is developing enhanced diagnostic capabilities for DMD. This project serves as a major diagnostic resource and is helping facilitate clinical trials in DMD by identifying patients who may be candidates for trials based on their molecular diagnosis.

Scientific Inquiry in the MD Research Community

NINDS has a strong focus on translational and clinical research in muscular dystrophy. Translational research is the process of applying ideas, insights, and discoveries generated through basic scientific inquiry into the treatment and prevention of disease. Four therapy development projects in muscular dystrophy have been funded through the NINDS Cooperative Program in Translational Research, a program designed to support milestone-driven projects focused on the identification and preclinical development of drugs, biologics, and devices in cell and animal models. Among the currently funded projects, there is a focus on development of a class of compounds known as protease inhibitors to combat muscle degeneration, on gene modification strategies to bypass mutations in the dystrophin gene, on combined gene modification and cell therapy approaches, and on bringing gene therapy for DMD to readiness for clinical trials. An additional project has been funded through the specialized program for translational research in muscular dystrophy that NINDS developed in conjunction with [other institutes]. This project is exploring strategies of gene delivery to all muscles in an arm or leg, thereby starting to bridge the gap between ongoing single muscle injection clinical trials and the ultimate need for systemic gene therapy delivery in patients. This new specialized program for translational research in muscular dystrophy has generated a strong response from the muscular dystrophy research community and NIH anticipates that further applications will be submitted through this program.

NINDS also funds two clinical trials in muscular dystrophy. The aim of the trial at the Columbus Children's Research Institute is to test the potential of gentamicin as a therapy for DMD and LGMD by "skipping over" or "reading through" mutations in the causative genes. A second trial at the University of Rochester is testing treatment with the growth factor complex IPlex in patients with myotonic dystrophy. NINDS is also funding a planning grant for a phase 3 [human efficacy] trial to identify optimal treatment regimens for corticosteroids in DMD.

National Institute of Arthritis and Musculoskeletal and Skin Diseases (NIAMS). NIAMS supports basic, translational and clinical studies on the muscular dystrophies and other muscle diseases and disorders. NIAMS funds considerable research to advance the understanding of the cellular and molecular mechanisms that underlie the muscle degeneration associated with the muscular dystrophies and to develop potential treatment strategies for these diseases. NIAMS supports basic research projects to study normal muscle development and pathophysiology of muscle disorders using animal models and cells from human subjects. Basic studies investigating the capacity of healthy muscle tissue to regenerate after injury have led to the identification and characterization of muscle stem cells and other cell types that can serve as precursors for muscle. NIAMS-supported investigators continue to advance the understanding of inflammatory components in several forms of muscular dystrophy and the role of the immune system in disease progression. Several groups of NIAMS-supported investigators have recently made significant advances in understanding the causes of myotonic dystrophy, which is an important step in developing treatments.

Discoveries from NIAMS-supported basic projects in muscle biology and disease have led to promising strategies for the treatment of muscular dystrophies including pharmacological, and gene- and cell-based therapies. NIAMS supports several translational research projects aimed at developing and testing recombinant viruses engineered to be vehicles for the delivery of therapeutic genes that may block or reverse muscle degeneration. For example, the Senator Paul D. Wellstone Cooperative Research Center at the University of Pittsburgh is exploring gene therapy and muscle derived stem cell therapies for the treatment of muscular dystrophies. Other areas of translational research include the identification and testing of potential drugs to block the enzymes that cause muscle degeneration and pharmacological methods to promote muscle growth. NIAMS supports studies of patients with LGMD, myotonic dystrophy, Emery-Dreifuss muscular dystrophy, and congenital muscular dystrophies, and facilitates clinical studies in myotonic dystrophy and FSHD through support of a registry of patient information, which is co-funded with NINDS.

> **FAST FACT**
>
> Muscular dystrophy can affect people of all ages. While some forms first become apparent in infancy or childhood, others may not appear until middle age or later.

One of the NIAMS-supported Wellstone Centers, involving researchers at the University of Pennsylvania, Johns Hopkins University and the NINDS intramural research program is preparing to conduct a clinical trial on the efficacy of a class of compounds known as protease inhibitors for DMD. Additionally, the Institute supports extensive research in other areas of muscle biology, which may point to targeted interventions for the treatment of muscular dystrophies and other disorders.

National Institute of Child Health and Human Development (NICHD). NICHD sponsors a portfolio of extramural research projects related to the muscular dystrophies and other neuromuscular disorders. Research topics related to muscular dystrophy are focused in two of the Institute's centers: the National Center for Medical Rehabilitation Research (NCMRR) and the Center for Developmental Biology and Perinatal Medicine (CDBPM).

The NCMRR is supporting several projects related to muscular dystrophy. Current research topics include development of non-invasive imaging to study loss and recovery of muscle strength and function, potential viral-mediated gene transfer to prevent disuse syndrome and accelerate restoration of function, and molecular characteristics of muscle remodeling in response to rehabilitation after immobilization. NCMRR is also interested in all aspects of exercise related to management of the muscular dystrophies.

Within CDBPM, the Mental Retardation and Developmental Disabilities Branch has supported research into cognitive disabilities in DMD and accepts applications for research on the nonskeletal manifestations of many of the muscular dystrophies. Areas of research interest also include nutrition and obesity in muscular dystrophy and family and psychosocial issues such as effects on other family members.

Newborn and Pediatric Research

In addition, NICHD is addressing issues related to newborn screening that are expected to have relevance to the muscular dystrophies and other neuromuscular disorders in the near future. NICHD released two sets of initiatives relevant to newborn screening. The purpose of the first, "Innovative Therapies and Clinical Studies for Screenable Disorders," is to improve the understanding and/or stimulate the development of therapeutic interventions for currently screened conditions and "high priority" genetic conditions for which investigators could potentially develop screening tests in the near future, including DMD. The second, "Novel Technologies in Newborn Screening," seeks to develop a multiplexed screening technology prototype for newborn screening, particularly for disorders with current or promising therapeutic interventions, like DMD. NICHD is also currently planning to develop a translational newborn screening research network to create a system which can translate the outcomes from these initiatives into clinical practice. . . .

Finally, NICHD also sponsors several networks that are available to support muscular dystrophy research and research training. These include the Pediatric Pharmacology Research Network, which is available for [conducting] trials of new pharmacotherapeutic agents. Two current trials are: "An Open-Label Pilot Study of Pentoxifylline in Steroid-Naive Duchenne Muscular Dystrophy," which seeks to estimate the magnitude and variability of muscle strength change for patients with DMD treated with pentoxifylline, a potent anti-inflammatory compound, and "A Randomized Study of Daily vs. High-dose Weekly Prednisone Therapy in Duchenne Muscular Dystrophy," a prospective, randomized study to compare efficacy and safety of two dose schedules of prednisone in boys with DMD.

The other relevant program is the Pediatric Scientist Training Program, which can contribute to the training of new young investigators. Both of these programs are managed through the Center for Research for Mothers and Children, another component of NICHD.

A New Technique May Aid in Diagnosis of Muscular Dystrophy

Heather Hare

The diagnosis of muscular dystrophy is generally a prolonged and expensive process. Since muscle weakness is the principal symptom and since it comes on slowly, it can easily be mistaken or overlooked. Even those with the most common form of the disease, Duchenne muscular dystrophy, are often not diagnosed until the disease is well established. In the selection that follows Heather Hare describes a blood test that may change all that. According to research conducted at the University of Rochester Medical Center, a simple test for the enzyme creatine kinase can indicate the presence of muscular dystrophy. Hare writes that use of such a screening test could facilitate early diagnosis and avoid costly tests and misdiagnoses. This could be especially important for identifying the disease in children whose parents never suspect the presence of muscular dystrophy. Hare reports that one-third of the two most common forms of muscular dystrophy occurred in boys without any family history of the disease. Hare is the assistant director of public relations and communications at the University of Rochester Medical Center in Rochester, New York.

Boys show signs of Duchenne Muscular Dystrophy (DMD) for 2 ½ years before they obtain a diagnosis and disease-specific treatment, about the same length of delay children have endured for the past 20 years despite advances in genetic testing and treatment. A simple and inexpensive blood test for any boy with symptoms and signs of motor delays and abnormalities could speed up the process while pilot studies on newborn screening are conducted.

Recent University of Rochester Medical Center research published in the *Journal of Pediatrics* shows that boys who are eventually diagnosed with DMD show signs of the disease for more than a year before families bring it to the attention of a health care provider. It takes another year before these children are screened with a serum CK test—a simple and inexpensive blood test for creatine kinase, an enzyme that leaks out of damaged muscle.

FAST FACT

Children who have Duchenne muscular dystrophy are typically diagnosed between the ages of three and five, much earlier than diagnoses for other forms of the disease.

An Affordable Shortcut

"The CK test is an easily available and cheap test," said Emma Ciafaloni, M.D., associate professor of Neurology at the University of Rochester Medical Center and author of the paper. "If they get the test and the diagnosis earlier, they can start treatment earlier and access the best care in the appropriate clinics and the best available services in their school. Early diagnosis will avoid unnecessary and costly tests and numerous unnecessary referrals to the wrong specialists. Parents and maternal relatives can also seek genetic counseling before they plan to have more children."

DMD, the most common muscular dystrophy in children is a particularly devastating form of the disease that affects 1 in 3,500 boys. It is an X-linked recessive genetic disease with onset of symptoms in boys between 2 and 6 years old. It progresses rapidly, rendering patients

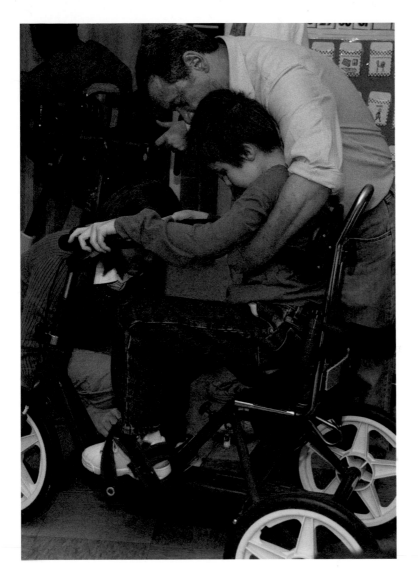

According to experts, Duchenne muscular dystrophy—the most common and the most devastating form of the disease in children—typically leads to reliance on a wheelchair by age ten or eleven. (Ellen B. Senisi/Photo Researchers, Inc.)

wheelchair bound by 10 or 11 years old. Most patients die in their mid–late 20s.

Family History Is No Guide

The Centers for Disease Control and Prevention–funded study analyzed medical records of 453 boys born since 1982 with DMD or Becker Muscular Dystrophy in the Muscular Dystrophy Surveillance, Tracking and Research Network

(MD STARnet). Of those, 156 boys had no known family history of muscular dystrophy. The first signs of the disease in those boys were seen at an average of 2 ½ years old, but the average age when families brought the signs to the attention of a health care provider was 3 ½ years old. The average age for children to receive the CK test or to see a neurologist was more than 4 ½ years old.

"We need to educate families to bring delays or abnormalities in motor skill—such as frequent falls, difficulty jumping, running or claiming stairs—to the attention of their health care providers as soon as they see them. And we need to educate pediatricians, family practitioners and all providers involved in the care of young children to recognize the early signs of DMD and to order a CK test if they see any motor delays or abnormalities," Ciafaloni said. "The sooner we start treatment, the more potential we have for delaying the disease's progression."

Scientists Are Closing In on the Genes That Cause Muscular Dystrophy

Tom Rickey

In 1992 scientists identified a particular genetic defect as responsible for one kind of muscular dystrophy known as the facioscapulohumeral variety. In the following selection science writer Tom Rickey announces a new breakthrough in muscular dystrophy research. He reports that scientists at the University of Rochester and their partners at other institutions have discovered how insufficient copies of a certain set of genes in muscular dystrophy patients leads to the disease. The scientists have fingerprinted a piece of DNA that was previously thought to be "junk"—an inactive segment. They say that the suspect DNA appears to become functional in people who have fewer copies of the genetic segment. The remaining task, the scientists say, is to figure out just how that suspect segment causes the disease. Rickey is a science writer employed by the University of Rochester Medical Center.

Nearly two decades after they identified the specific genetic flaw that causes a common type of muscular dystrophy, scientists believe they have figured out how that flaw brings about the disease. The finding by an international team of researchers settles a longstanding question about the roots of facioscapulohumeral muscular dystrophy, or FSHD. The work was published online August 19 [2010] in *Science*.

Unraveling how the genetic defect causes FSHD has been especially challenging for scientists. Unlike with many genetic diseases, their identification of the mutation that is the basis of FSHD didn't quickly lead to a deeper understanding of how the disease actually comes about. That lack of clarity has posed a significant barrier to researchers hoping to turn the knowledge of the genetic flaw into significant progress for patients.

A New Target for Therapy

The latest findings clarify the picture significantly. Scientists have discovered that several deleted versions of a gene trigger the remaining copies of that gene to be much more active than usual. That's because the DNA that codes for the gene is not as tightly coiled or elusive to the body's molecular machinery as usual when some copies are missing, and so the gene—known as DUX4, which makes a protein harmful to muscle cells—is more active than it should be.

The work offers up a new therapeutic target to scientists aiming to develop a treatment or cure for the disease.

"It is amazing to realize that a long and frustrating journey of almost two decades now culminates in the identification of a single small DNA variant that differs between patients and people without the disease. We finally have a target that we can go after," says Silvère van der Maarel, professor of medical epigenetics at the University of Leiden in the Netherlands.

FSHD is an inherited disorder that usually makes its presence felt in the teen years. First symptoms usually are

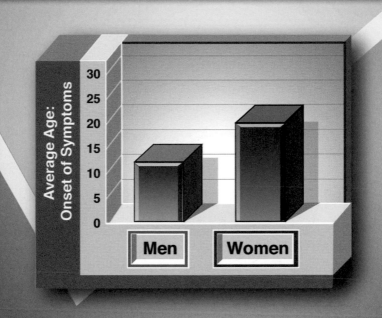

Average Age at the Onset of Facioscapulohumeral Muscular Dystrophy

Average Age: Onset of Symptoms

30
25
20
15
10
5
0

Men   Women

Taken from: Facioscapulohumeral Muscular Dystrophy Society, "Facts and Statistics About FSHD," www.fshsociety.org.

weakness in the upper body; for example, a person might have trouble lifting the arms. Weakness of the facial muscles is also common; for instance, difficulty smiling or whistling, closing the eyelids completely, or even sipping through a straw. Later on, the condition affects the lower body—the muscles of the feet, legs, and hips. Patients usually live a normal life span, but around 20 percent of patients end up using a wheelchair.

Genetic Deficiency from Scientists' Perspective

Doctors estimate that about 1 in 20,000 people worldwide, including about 15,000 Americans, have FSHD, which is the third most common type of muscular dystrophy. It was . . . in 1992, that a team from the same laboratory in Leiden identified the genetic defect at the

Spontaneous mutations in utero

30%

70%

Inheritance from a parent

Taken from: Facioscapulohumeral Muscular Dystrophy Society, "Facts and Statistics About FSHD," www.fshsociety.org.

root of the disease. The scientists found that in healthy people there are 11 or more copies of a certain DNA sequence dubbed D4Z4 near the tip on chromosome 4. Nearly all FSHD patients have too-few copies—10 or fewer of the D4Z4 repeat. Since then the team has worked to understand how that defect translates into the disease.

"In most patients with FSHD, a piece of DNA is missing," says Rabi Tawil, professor of neurology at the University of Rochester and a co-author of the paper. "For a long time it was thought that this was simply junk DNA that was missing, and that the missing material must affect the function of a nearby gene on chromosome 4."

It turns out that each of the D4Z4 repeats contains a copy of a gene known as DUX4, but scientists have not known until recently that DUX4 is a functional gene. When a critical number of copies are missing, the structure of the tip of chromosome 4 becomes more open, making the DUX4 gene more accessible for transcription. When crucial pieces of DNA that introduce and conclude the repetitive string are composed of certain sequences, the ingredients for molecular mischief are in place, making the remaining copies of DUX4 much more stable than they normally are.

The University of Rochester has been involved in both clinical and translational research, creating the National Registry of Myotonic and FSHD Patients and Family Members, which includes information on hundreds of patients who volunteer for research. Rochester has also has established the world's largest repository of biological samples, such as blood, skin, and muscle specimens, from individuals with FSHD.

The current research "provides a new and unifying model for FSHD because it will focus future research on determining whether the DUX4 protein causes FSHD, as indicated by our consortium's genetic analysis," says Stephen Tapscott, of the Fred Hutchinson Cancer Research Center.

Still No Treatment

The team is currently studying how active DUX4 is in patients in FSHD compared to people who do not have the disease.

In previous research, other investigators had identified a nearby gene known as FRG1 as central to the development of FSHD. Researchers were unable to reproduce those results and instead point to DUX4.

> **FAST FACT**
>
> Researchers have found that gene DUX4 is abundantly expressed in egg and sperm cells.

Currently there is no treatment for FSHD that slows the disease or addresses the underlying problem. Typically patients are treated with medications to alleviate their pain, and are given supportive treatment, such as braces and other aids for their arms and legs to help them deal with weakness. There have been a few studies investigating possible treatments—drugs on the market for other conditions—but those haven't turned up anything that works in FSHD patients.

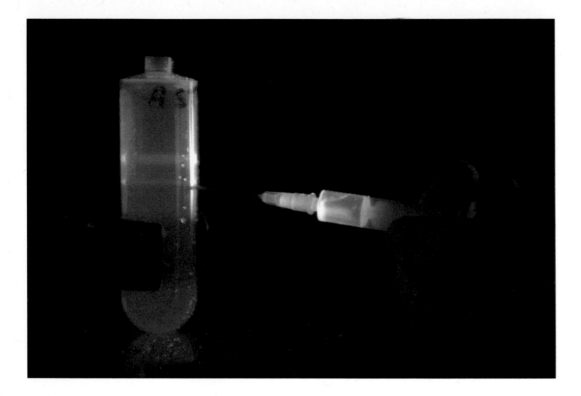

DNA testing has revealed that most people with facioscapulohumeral muscular dystrophy have a small segment of DNA missing from their genetic makeup. (© Patrick Landmann/ Photo Researchers, Inc.)

"Interventions tried thus far haven't been based on the science underlying the disease," Tawil says. "That's why this is such an exciting step. Instead of guesswork, we now have one unified hypothesis, and one target. This marks the first time we can work solidly from basic science to seek a treatment for FSHD."

The team plans to screen existing compounds in a search for one that inhibits DUX4. The group also plans to develop rigorous techniques for measuring the effects of test medications on FSHD patients, and to continue to try to understand how DUX4 damages muscles. Early research indicates that DUX4 hinders the body's ability to regenerate muscle and makes muscles more susceptible to oxidative stress.

Researchers from the University of Washington, Nice University in [France], and the Radboud University in the Netherlands contributed to the research.

Drug Therapy Gives Cautious Optimism for Treating Muscular Dystrophy

Matthew Herper

Bad grammar or poor punctuation can cause miscommunication in writing. In the following selection journalist Matthew Herper reports on a drug that shows promise in combating the effects of "bad grammar and punctuation" in genes. Duchenne muscular dystrophy, the most common kind, is caused by misspellings and misplaced "punctuation marks" in the genome. The mistakes are known as nonsense mutations. The Duchenne variety of the disease seems to respond to an experimental drug developed by the biotech company PTC Therapeutics, Herper reports; however, researchers are reluctant to draw broad conclusions. Experience has shown that trials often show promise only to disappoint later. If the drug does come through the trials successfully, it may be applicable to some other diseases caused by nonsense mutations, he says. Herper is a science and business reporter at *Forbes* magazine.

SOURCE: Matthew Herper, "Stopping the Nonsense," *Forbes,* September 17, 2007. Reprinted by permission of Forbes Media, LLC Copyright © 2011.

Matthew DeRiggi is 9 years old and plays basketball every day. But by the time he's a teenager he likely will be unable even to walk. He will need a wheelchair, then a ventilator, and odds are he won't survive his 30s as his muscles fail him, his lungs fail to inflate and his heart eventually is unable to keep beating. Matt is one of 13,000 boys in the U.S. who have a rare form of muscular dystrophy known as Duchenne.

"We're doing everything we can to keep Matt healthy for as long as we can," says his mom, Barbara DeRiggi. "You have to realize there is no cure out there, and you have to do as much as you can to find one."

She has new hope, however, for an experimental drug made by an unknown New Jersey biotech called PTC Therapeutics. It has helped Matt after only one month of treatment. Though he can play sports, he has needed help getting out of the family car for a few years; the first time he did it recently without having to take her hand, "I thought, 'Oh my God, it's working,'" DeRiggi says.

Richard Finkel, Matt's doctor at Children's Hospital of Philadelphia, says the drug seems to help other kids temporarily, but he cautions that parents can be fooled by hope. Duchenne muscular dystrophy, discovered by French neurologist Guillaume Duchenne in 1868, accounts for 40% of the cases of muscular dystrophy in the U.S. In 1987 it became one of the first ailments linked to a defect in a particular gene, but since then the main treatments have been limited and unable to halt the disease's devastating effects.

PTC Therapeutics' drug, which just completed midstage trials in 38 boys, aims beyond treating symptoms to target what went wrong in the gene that triggered the MD malady. Moreover, while the patient base for Duchenne may be too small to spark a billion-dollar drug, the PTC chemical could work against similar underlying gene flaws in other disorders, such as cystic fibrosis, he-

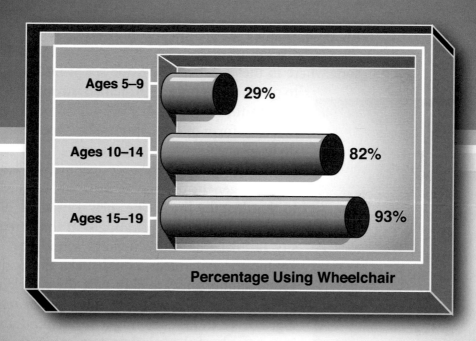

Wheelchair Use for Boys and Young Men with MD

A Centers for Disease Control and Prevention survey of boys with either Duchenne or Becker muscular dystrophy finds that wheelchair use increases dramatically with age.

Ages 5–9   29%

Ages 10–14   82%

Ages 15–19   93%

Percentage Using Wheelchair

Taken from: Centers for Disease Control and Prevention, "Prevalence of Duchenne Becker Muscular Dystrophy Among Males Aged 5–24 Years—Four States, 2007," *Morbidity and Mortality Weekly Report*, vol. 58, no. 40, October 16, 2009.

mophilia and spinal muscular atrophy. A separate PTC trial involves 47 patients with CF.

Duchenne is caused by misspellings in the gene that tells the body to produce a protein called dystrophin, a glue that helps hold muscle tissue together. This one gene is the longest of the 25,000 that make up the human genome, and it consists of 2.2 million "letters" (A, T, G and C for four different nucleic acids), which spell out the recipe for making the muscle protein. A single misplaced

A Popular Nutritional Supplement May Aid in Treatment of Muscular Dystrophy

Jared P. Pearlman and Roger A. Fielding

Nutritional supplements are minimally regulated, over-the-counter products. Unlike prescription drugs, supplements do not have to pass scientific tests to prove their efficacy. Many of them are sold with extravagant claims. None of this means, however, that a nutritional supplement cannot do some good, according to Jared P. Pearlman and Roger A. Fielding in the following selection. The authors introduce a controversial supplement that appears to be helpful to those who suffer from Duchenne muscular dystrophy. Creatine became popular among athletes in the 1990s for its reported muscle-building effects. Pearlman and Fielding report that more recently researchers have begun investigating the supplement's potential to rebuild wasted muscles in Duchenne or Becker muscular dystrophy patients. The authors cite a study that found a 25 percent increase in muscle power among patients who took the supplement. They also cite evidence that creatine helps build fat-free body mass in such patients and may improve the condition of their bones. How it does this, however, remains unclear, and more study is necessary, the authors say. Fielding is the senior scientist and director of the Jean Mayer USDA Human Nutrition Research Center at Tufts University in Boston. His collaborator, Pearlman, earned a bachelor's of science degree at Tufts and worked under Fielding.

SOURCE: Jared P. Pearlman and Roger A. Fielding, "Creatine Monohydrate as a Therapeutic Aid in Muscular Dystrophy," *Nutrition Reviews,* February 2006. Copyright © 2006 by John Wiley & Sons. Reproduced by permission.

The widespread popularity of creatine supplementation among athletes has prompted scientists to examine other uses for this important metabolic compound. [Researcher M.A.] Tarnopolsky et al. recently reported on the potential therapeutic effects of creatine supplementation in individuals suffering from Duchenne's muscular dystrophy (DMD). These results support previous findings that creatine may alleviate symptoms of muscular dystrophy and, when used in conjunction with corticosteroids, can significantly reduce the amount of atrophy associated with the progression of this debilitating disease. The present review provides an overview of creatine metabolism, dietary sources, and effects on physical performance, as well as summarizes and reviews the results of recent work suggesting that creatine may have benefits in specific neuromuscular diseases such as muscular dystrophy.

Sources of Creatine

Creatine is an amino acid derivative formed from arginine and glycine via two enzymatic reactions. Guanidinoacetate is formed in the kidney and is transferred to the liver, where it is methylated to form creatine. . . . Creatine is also obtained through the diet, with intake largely dependent on average daily meat and poultry consumption. . . . When food is digested, creatine enters the bloodstream and is delivered to skeletal muscle, where it can be used for energy production. . . . Most, if not all, of the creatine synthesized in the body, and that which is exogenously consumed, is excreted by the kidney in the form of creatinine. . . .

How Creatine Works

Creatine exerts its effects on metabolism by serving as a precursor to the formation of ATP [adenosine triphosphate]. When energy demands increase, phosphocreatine donates its phosphate group to ADP [adenosine diphosphate] to form ATP via the creatine kinase (CK) reaction. CK has been identified as an isozyme that functions in two opposing ways. One form of CK, mitochondrial CK, catalyzes phosphocreatine synthesis from ATP generated by oxidative phosphorylation. Conversely, cytosolic CK catalyzes the regeneration of ATP from phosphocreatine at specific sites of ATP consumption. When mutants lacking mitochondrial CK were initially examined, few phenotypic [outward] changes were observed. However, when researchers began distinguishing between the CKs specific to muscle and those specific to other organ systems, certain abnormalities were discovered. Mice deficient in muscle CK exhibited characteristics usually found in dystrophic mice, such as decreased muscular force, power, work, and maximal voluntary contraction. . . .

Creatine's Role in Exercise

The use of creatine to enhance athletic performance has been widely studied but remains relatively inconclusive. Since the phosphocreatine/creatine pathway is involved with ATP production under anaerobic [not involving oxygen] conditions, the majority of studies have dealt with the acute effects of creatine supplementation on the intensity, duration, and frequency of exercise. Studies suggest that the beneficial effects of oral creatine ingestion can be seen with a dose of approximately 20 g/d [grams per day] of creatine for 5 to 7 days. At higher exercise intensities, the effect of creatine supplementation would depend on the increase in phosphocreatine levels relative to the ATP turnover rate. Of the positive results that have been obtained during acute bouts of creatine supplementation, researchers have shown increases in fat-free muscle mass and maximal strength while prolonging physical activity by decreasing lactate accumulation. . . .

The effects of long-term creatine supplementation on athletic performance are largely speculative, although studies have shown some positive results. [Researcher

K.] Vandenberghe et al. studied the effects of creatine supplementation in women who performed a resistance training program that included seven different exercises: leg press, bench press, leg curl, leg extension, squat, shoulder press, and sit-ups. The results showed increases in muscle phosphocreatine, strength, intermittent exercise capacity, and fat-free mass in the group who was given creatine for 10 weeks. Compared with placebo, 4 days of high-dose creatine ingestion (20 g/d) followed by 10 weeks of low-dose creatine intake (2 g/d) increased maximal strength, maximal intermittent exercise capacity, and fat-free mass by 20% to 25%, 10% to 25%, and 60%, respectively. However, [researcher L.J.C.] Van Loon et al. found that prolonged creatine supplementation (20 g/d for 5 days and 2 g/d for 6 weeks) did not increase oxidative capacity or performance during endurance cycling, but did increase fat-free mass. More conclusive studies are needed to address the efficacy of long-term creatine supplementation. . . .

> **FAST FACT**
>
> On average, muscular dystrophy patients increased muscle strength by 8.5 percent from supplementing with creatine.

Creatine for Treatment of Muscular Dystrophy

Few studies, however, have looked at the human response to creatine as a therapeutic agent in alleviating the symptoms of muscular dystrophy. Results from the few published studies dealing with creatine and muscular dystrophy are contradictory. [Researcher M.C.] Walter et al. showed little to no benefit of creatine supplementation in patients with myotonic and muscular dystrophies. In contrast, other researchers have found positive benefits of creatine in dystrophic patients. [Researcher M.] Louis et al. showed that patients with DMD or Becker's muscular dystrophy receiving creatine (3 g/d for 3 months) increased their maximal voluntary contraction by 25% and almost doubled their time to fatigue.

A recent study by Tarnopolsky et al. reported on the benefits of creatine supplementation in patients with DMD. This is the first long-term human study that examines the effects of exogenous [supplemental] creatine on motor function and muscle strength in DMD patients, some of whom were using corticosteroids. The study assessed the degree to which corticosteroid use would affect the results of creatine supplementation in these patients and whether creatine could safely be used in conjunction with corticosteroid therapy.

The investigators performed a double-blind, placebo-controlled, cross-over study in which 30 participants were randomized to one of two groups. One group was given creatine and the other group was assigned to a placebo. Of the 15 subjects who were taking corticosteroids, 13 were using deflazacort and two were using prednisone. Three of the 30 subjects required a wheelchair for mobility. After 4 months of creatine or placebo treatment, there was a washout period of 6 weeks. The subjects were then switched to the opposite treatment for another 4 months. The creatine supplement was given in the form of a chewable tablet. . . . The placebo was also in tablet form and was given to the subjects in an identical number each day. Although corticosteroid use has been shown to improve function in DMD, the randomized cross-over design and the addition of corticosteroids as a factor in these statistical models eliminated this potential confounder.

Strength measurements were assessed by manual muscle testing and were graded based on the investigator's own grading scale. Maximal isometric handgrip strength was determined using a dynamometer for the dominant and non-dominant hands. Peak strength from three trials was recorded. The investigators also used a custom-made force transducer to measure handgrip strength, which was then correlated with peak strength as tested with the dynamometer. Participants were also subjected to a dual energy X-ray absorptiometry (DEXA)

scan to determine fat-free mass, percent body fat, bone mineral content, and bone mineral density. Functional testing was performed on the subjects and included [the] time [it took them] to: 1) walk or wheel 30 feet; 2) climb four stairs; 3) stand from a supine position; and 4) cut a 3´3-inch square from an 8×11-inch piece of paper. . . .

A recent study has reported on the benefits of using a creatine supplement in treating patients with Duchenne muscular dystrophy. (© Ian Patrick/Alamy)

Some Promising Results

Results from the strength and functional testing showed that creatine could improve some motor function in patients with DMD irrespective of corticosteroid use. Handgrip strength increased in the dominant hand and the non-dominant hand, but the increase in non-dominant hand strength was not statistically significant. Manual muscle strength decreased more in the placebo group (3.7% loss) than in the creatine group (2.8% loss), but these results were also not statistically significant. No significant changes were seen in activities of daily living, functional testing, or pulmonary function.

The effects of creatine on body composition showed an increase in fat-free mass during the creatine phase when collapsed across corticosteroid treatment. Mean percent body fat was lower in the creatine phase, but the results were not statistically significant. These data suggest that creatine does increase fat-free mass and may attenuate increases in percent body fat in patients with DMD; however, the mechanism of these changes is not clear. It is speculated that creatine's hyperosmotic effect [increased pressure] in cells could produce a phenotypic change, but this has yet to be determined. . . .

A Possible Alternative to Corticosteroids

These results provide some of the first evidence that creatine is a safe therapeutic aid in treating symptoms of DMD and, most importantly, that these effects are independent of corticosteroid therapy. Corticosteroids have long been used in treating symptoms of muscular dystrophy because of their anabolic effect, but the side effects are problematic. Patients using corticosteroids show increases in strength, which can last from months to years. The addition of creatine to corticosteroid therapy could result in even more strength gains and maintenance of muscle mass. The authors view these results as promising, and mention that "in combination with our recent findings that creatine attenuated corticosteroid-induced growth retardation in rats, these findings are potentially of therapeutic benefit for the many growing children with DMD who are taking corticosteroids."

Tarnopolsky et al. cite two reasons that it was important to show that the beneficial effects of creatine were independent of corticosteroid use. For one, creatine may provide an alternative therapy to corticosteroids, thus reducing the risk of unwanted side effects. Secondly, in those patients who have been taking corticosteroids for some time, creatine may produce an additive effect; however, this was not well tested in the study. Thus, it may be of interest to perform a dose-response study in humans testing the effects of various doses of corticosteroids and creatine used in conjunction with one another, and then compare these results to those obtained in the Tarnopolsky study. . . .

Compelling Data

The most compelling data from this study were the reported increase in both fat-free mass and strength in response to creatine. . . .

Tarnopolsky et al. have laid the groundwork for future studies examining creatine supplementation and its potential role as a therapeutic agent in muscular dystrophy, though the mechanism(s) by which creatine may increase fat-free mass and strength remains largely unknown. Additional studies are needed to elucidate the role of this important metabolic intermediate on the control of skeletal muscle growth in patients with neuromuscular disease. In these studies, sufficient numbers of subjects will need to be enrolled in trials of longer duration to accurately assess the degree to which creatine can provide musculoskeletal and neuroprotective effects.

CHAPTER 2

Issues and Controversies Concerning Muscular Dystrophy

Stem Cell Therapy Has Not Produced Cures for Diseases Such as Muscular Dystrophy

Emily Yoffe

Stem cell therapy is part of a larger field known as regenerative medicine, which includes a variety of gene therapies. In the selection that follows Emily Yoffe critiques the entire field of gene therapy, including stem cell therapy. There have been extravagant promises made, she says, but few have been kept. Stem cells promise to replace damaged tissues, such as muscle destroyed by muscular dystrophy, but the applications to date have been not only disappointing but downright dangerous, Yoffe says. She cites a case in which a boy in Russia was treated with stem cells that, instead of curing him, created tumors in his body. Yoffe is a journalist who writes frequently for *Slate*, an online magazine.

D r. J. William Langston [founder of the Parkinson's Institute] has been researching Parkinson's disease for 25 years. At one time, it seemed likely he'd have to find another disease to study, because a cure for Parkinson's looked imminent. In the late 1980s, the

Photo on facing page. Gene therapy has been found to help muscular dystrophy patients improve through the injection of genes. The procedure is useful in treating the disease, but many challenges remain in the search for treatments and a cure. (© PHANIE/Photo Researchers, Inc.)

field of regenerative medicine seemed poised to make it possible for doctors to put healthy tissue in a damaged brain, reversing the destruction caused by the disease.

Langston was one of many optimists. In 1999, the then-head of the National Institute of Neurological Disorders and Stroke, Dr. Gerald Fischbach, testified before the Senate that with "skill and luck," Parkinson's could be cured in five to 10 years. Now Langston, who is 67, doesn't think he'll see a Parkinson's cure in his professional lifetime. He no longer uses "the C word" and acknowledges he and others were naive. He understands the anger of patients who, he says, "are getting quite bitter" that they remain ill, long past the time when they thought they would have been restored to health.

Big Promises, Small Payoff

The disappointments are so acute in part because the promises have been so big. Over the past two decades, we've been told that a new age of molecular medicine—using gene therapy, stem cells, and the knowledge gleaned from unlocking the human genome—would bring us medical miracles. Just as antibiotics conquered infectious diseases and vaccines eliminated the scourges of polio and smallpox, the ability to manipulate our cells and genes is supposed to vanquish everything from terrible inherited disorders, such as Huntington's and cystic fibrosis, to widespread conditions like cancer, diabetes, and heart disease.

Adding to the frustration is an endless stream of laboratory animals that are always getting healed. Mice with Parkinson's have been successfully treated with stem cells, as have mice with sickle cell anemia. Dogs with hemophilia and muscular dystrophy have been made disease-free. But humans keep experiencing suffering and death. Why? What explains the tremendous mismatch between expectation and reality? Are the cures really coming, just more slowly than expected? Or have scientists fundamentally misled us, and themselves, about the potential of new medical technologies? . . .

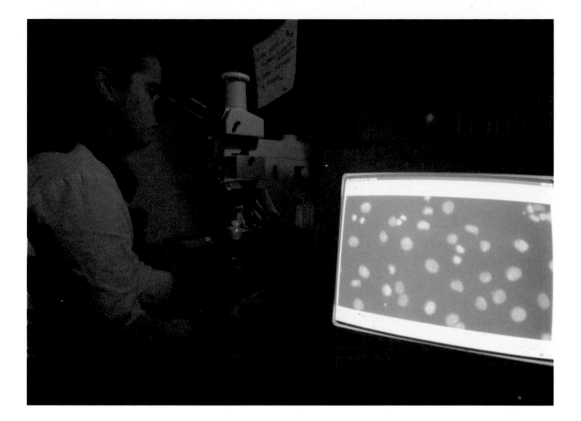

Still in the Experimental Stage

Gene therapy remains [in 2010] experimental 20 years after its first human trials because of a series of vexing problems. For one thing, the new gene has to get to the right place and continue working—without causing any unwanted side effects. In 1999, 18-year-old Jesse Gelsinger became a pivotal figure in gene therapy, an unintended martyr. Gelsinger suffered from a genetic liver disorder, though he had a mild case that could be treated with drugs. He volunteered for experimental gene therapy to correct it. A few hours after receiving a transfusion of normal genes delivered inside a cold virus, he became feverish; within days, he was dead of massive organ failure. His death set back the entire field and ended the hope that curing disease by manipulating genes would be simple and safe.

A researcher studies stem cell nuclei under a light microscope. Critics say that research into the use of stem cells as a means of treating muscular dystrophy and other diseases has not been as productive as was previously hoped. (© **Pasquale Sorrentino/ Photo Researchers, Inc.**)

But scientists kept at it. In some ways, gene therapy for boys with a deadly immune disorder, X-linked severe combined immune deficiency, also known as "bubble boy" disease, is the miracle made manifest. Inserting good genes into these children has allowed some to live normal lives. Unfortunately, within a few years of treatment, a significant minority have developed leukemia. The gene therapy, it turns out, activated existing cancer-causing genes in these children. This results in what the co-discoverer of the structure of DNA, James Watson, calls "the depressing calculus" of curing an invariably fatal disease—and hoping it doesn't cause a sometimes-fatal one.

FAST FACT

Researchers believe that Duchenne muscular dystrophy, the most common type, is essentially a disease of stem cell failure.

Stem Cells Pose Risks

Then there are stem cells, which tantalize with their myriad possibilities: allowing diabetics to throw away their insulin, growing healthy cardiac tissue after a heart attack, restoring function to people with spinal cord injury (for which the Food and Drug Administration just approved the first embryonic stem cell trial). Embryonic stem cells—the subject of so much controversy—were first cultured in the lab a little more than a decade ago; in 2006, there was another breakthrough when adult cells were coaxed into becoming induced pluripotent stem cells. (Bone marrow transplants use adult stem cells, a treatment that has been used for decades.) But getting stem cells to work in the human body is neither an easy nor necessarily benign process. Researchers are concerned that stem cells, once let loose, might take a wrong turn; heart cells, for instance, could end up in the brain. They could also proliferate excessively, causing damage to nearby tissues. They could generate tumors. These aren't just hypotheticals. Doctors in Moscow injected neural embryonic stem cells into the brain and spinal fluid of a boy suffering from a rare, disabling, inherited disease, ataxia telangiectasia. The good news is that the transplanted cells persisted. The bad news is that they weren't effective in treating his disease. The worse news is the transplanted cells caused tumors in the boy's brain and spine.

The researchers who analyzed the boy's case acknowledge that any bold, new therapy for devastating diseases often carries grave risks. As Francis Collins [the director of the National Institutes of Health] says, "I'm very excited for the potential of stem cells," but adds, "We have to be very careful." He's careful enough not to venture a timetable as to when their potential will reach patients. . . .

Disappointments for Genetic Research

The *New York Times* recently pointed out that 10 years after the first draft of the human genome was announced, the hoped-for ability to identify the genetic causes of our major killers such as cancer and heart disease has been mostly a bust. Dozens, even hundreds, of potential gene variations have been linked to the diseases. As such mutations frequently fail to predict who falls ill, scientists wonder whether some once-promising gene associations could be simply coincidences. Yet even knowing exactly which mutated gene causes a disease—as in Huntington's and cystic fibrosis—doesn't necessarily mean it is either preventable or curable.

Sometimes our expanding knowledge does reveal new avenues for therapeutic interventions, as it also taunts with its complexity. Dr. Bruce Stillman, president of the Cold Spring Harbor Laboratory, says medical progress would be stuck without the advancements made in molecular biology over the past 40 years. He cites the successes of Herceptin for breast cancer and Gleevec for chronic myeloid leukemia, two drugs made possible by our growing understanding of how cells work. We've also learned, he says, that cancer is not one disease but many subtypes, so there will never be a

Incidence Rate for Leading Forms of Muscular Dystrophy

Duchenne MD: 1 in 3,300 live male births

Becker MD: 1 in 18,000 live male births

Facioscapulohumeral MD: 1 in 20,000 live births
(Males are more affected than are females.)

Each ▢ represents 127 live male births

Each ■ represents 692 live male births

Each ▢ represents 769 live male births

Taken from: Virtual Medical Centre, "Statistics on Muscular Dystrophy," July 2, 2008. www.virtualmedicalcentre.com.

single penicillin-like cure. "If anything, cancer has become a bigger problem because of the nature of our understanding," Stillman says.

The day is approaching when getting one's genome sequenced will cost only a few thousand dollars. Already, Glenn Close, Henry Louis Gates Jr., and a poodle named Shadow have had theirs done. Collins says this will be a crucial part of everyone's medical record, allowing us to see what dangers lurk in our genes. But Dr. David Goldstein, director of Duke University's Center for Human Genome Variation, says, "Right now we know very, very little of the genetics of the diseases that most people will get."

Gene Therapy Offers Hopeful Treatment Possibilities for Muscular Dystrophy

Amanda Gardner

Muscular dystrophy is a genetic disease, and many researchers place hopes in gene therapy to treat it. In the following selection journalist Amanda Gardner reports on a minor but potentially important breakthrough: Investigators at the University of Rochester Medical Center have managed to employ gene therapy to revive useless muscles in human subjects. Prior research had only succeeded in animal studies. Researchers injected fresh genes into patients suffering from limb-girdle muscular dystrophy to replace their faulty ones. The patients showed long-lasting improvements as a result. Other researchers are attempting to replicate and refine the results. Gardner is a reporter for HealthDay, a medical and health news service for both consumers and medical professionals.

This is the first time such a feat has been performed in humans, state the authors [of a study at the University of Rochester Medical Center], who are presenting their findings at the [2010] annual meeting of the American Society of Gene & Cell Therapy in Washington, D.C.

"This study provides additional information regarding the feasibility of gene therapy for the treatment of muscular dystrophy," said Dr. Valerie Cwik, executive vice president and research and medical director of the Muscular Dystrophy Association, which helped fund the research. "Specifically, it provides proof of principle, in people, for sustained gene expression [for at least six months] following treatment."

"This study has shown that a normal gene packed into a virus and injected directly into a muscle can actually produce the protein that is either defective or missing in this particular form of muscular dystrophy," added Dr. Rabi Tawil, a professor of neurology at the University of Rochester Medical Center. "Similar studies have been done in animal models, and this is the first to show a similar result in humans."

Hope for Extending Lives

If replicated, the findings could provide hope for people with this and other forms of muscular dystrophy.

> **FAST FACT**
>
> The first US trial on human subjects of a gene therapy for muscular dystrophy got under way in March 2006.

"Reversing or significantly blunting the severity of this weakness and wasting will give these patients major improvement in their quality of life, enhance their independence, and increase the likelihood that they can obtain employment," said Dr. Richard Moxley, director of the Neuromuscular Disease Center, also at the University of Rochester Medical Center.

The patients in this study had limb-girdle muscular dystrophy (LGMD), which is characterized by muscle weakness around the hips and shoulders. The condition results from an inherited deficiency of alpha-sarcoglycan, a muscle protein.

"There is no effective therapy to prevent the progressive weakness and loss of muscle that occurs in LGMD

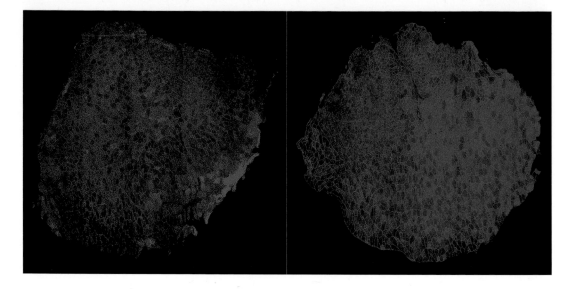

A light micrograph of a mouse forelimb is shown before (left) and after gene therapy. The mouse has an abnormal gene that reduces dystrophin production, which causes muscle loss. (© Patrick Landmann/ Photo Researchers, Inc.)

type 2D," Moxley explained. "The disease typically begins between 2 and 15 years of age, and many patients become wheelchair-bound by their teens. They have marked weakness of their shoulder and thigh muscles, and have difficulty performing many of the activities of daily life."

"Treatments are needed urgently," stated Cwik.

A previous study of the same gene transfer procedure had been successful in three patients with levels of the protein staying elevated for at least three months after treatment.

Injections of Healthy Genes

Here, a prominent group of muscular dystrophy researchers from the Center for Gene Therapy at the Research Institute at Nationwide Children's Hospital in Columbus, Ohio, injected three LGMD patients with a healthy gene, which succeeded in increasing both gene expression and muscle fiber levels. The effect persisted for six months, the longest yet.

Next, the researchers hope to inject the gene directly into a leg artery to see if those muscles will take up and use the protein.

But several obstacles remain.

"For gene therapy to be clinically beneficial—meaning an improvement in strength—multiple muscle groups will need to be treated simultaneously," Cwik said. "To do this will require regional [e.g., to an entire limb] or systemic delivery [to the entire body, such as intravenously]."

"This technique delivers the gene directly into the muscle through a needle. It is not practical to do this on large muscles, let alone several muscles, as it would require hundreds of injections," Tawil added. "To make this treatment viable, a system has to be devised where the virus-plus-normal gene can be injected into the circulation and have it deposited into all the muscles. The other obstacle is making sure that injecting the virus containing the normal gene does not induce the immune system to attack the virus."

Also, Cwik said, "We do not know if sustained gene expression will continue for much longer periods of time."

Gene Therapy Has Challenges to Overcome Before It Can Effectively Treat Muscular Dystrophy

Nationwide Children's Hospital

Gene therapy has appeared to be a promising avenue for treating muscular dystrophy, which is caused by faulty genes. In animal studies, replacement of the faulty genes has brought good results; however, in the selection that follows the staff of the Nationwide Children's Hospital report that research done there has revealed that gene therapy has obstacles to overcome if it is to prove effective in humans. Researchers at the hospital injected corrective genes into several boys suffering from muscular dystrophy. The genes were packaged within viruses that had been specially adapted to deliver them into the boys' muscle cells, but researchers were surprised to discover that some of the boys developed an immunity to the dystrophin that the new genes produced. Dystrophin is a key protein that is missing in muscular dystrophy patients. The immune reaction has so far thwarted the gene therapy, but scientists hope that by identifying the problem they will prompt others to resolve it. The Nationwide Children's Hospital is a pediatric research and treatment institution based in Columbus, Ohio.

SOURCE: Nationwide Children's Hospital, "Gene Therapy Reveals Unexpected Immunity to Dystrophin in Patients with Duchenne Muscular Dystrophy," October 6, 2010. Copyright © 2010 by Nationwide Children's Hospital. All rights reserved. Reprinted by permission.

An immune reaction to dystrophin, the muscle protein that is defective in patients with Duchenne muscular dystrophy, may pose a new challenge to strengthening muscles of patients with this disease, suggests a new study appearing in the October 7, 2010, issue of *The New England Journal of Medicine.*

Duchenne muscular dystrophy (DMD) is a hereditary and lethal neuromuscular disease characterized by progressive loss of muscle strength and integrity. Genetic information important for production of a functional dystrophin protein is deleted from the DMD gene of many patients. Studies by investigators at Nationwide Children's Hospital have examined the possibility of improving muscle strength by using modified viruses to deliver a corrected copy of the DMD gene to patients' muscles.

Dystrophin Fails to Appear Long-Term

"DMD genes packaged into viral vectors [carriers] strengthen muscles in mouse models of muscular dystrophy," said Jerry R. Mendell, MD, director, Center for Gene Therapy at The Research Institute at Nationwide Children's Hospital and one of the study authors. "In this study we attempted to translate basic research from the animal model to patients with DMD." Six boys with DMD gene deletions were treated by injecting a viral vector containing a corrected DMD gene into the biceps muscle of one arm. However, when the patients were evaluated three months later, long-term production of dystrophin protein from the corrected DMD gene was not detected.

"With one safety trial involving six patients, Drs. Mendell and [Christopher] Walker have provided a tremendous service to scientists advancing gene therapy research—particularly for muscular dystrophy," said Louis M. Kunkel, Ph.D., chairman of the Muscular Dystrophy Association (MDA) Scientific Advisory Committee. "By uncovering a somewhat surprising T cell immune response

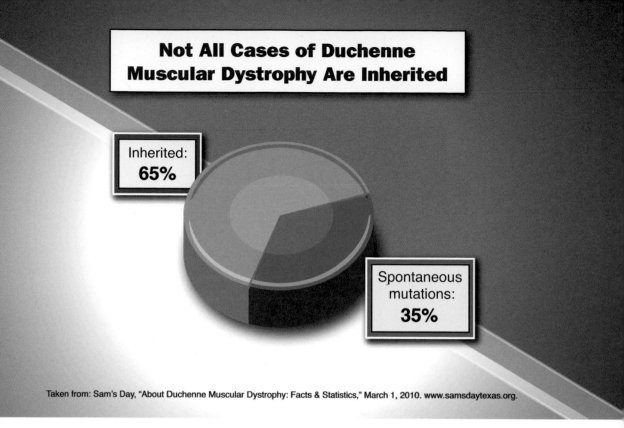

Not All Cases of Duchenne Muscular Dystrophy Are Inherited

Inherited:
65%

Spontaneous mutations:
35%

Taken from: Sam's Day, "About Duchenne Muscular Dystrophy: Facts & Statistics," March 1, 2010. www.samsdaytexas.org.

to dystrophin, they're helping investigators refine several distinct and promising approaches to treating Duchenne muscular dystrophy (DMD) by correcting or adding the dystrophin protein that is defective in the disease."

Corrected Genes Appear Foreign

To understand why this therapy failed, the researchers measured immune responses against dystrophin. "We were concerned about immunity caused by a certain type of white blood cell called the T lymphocyte. The natural role of T cells is to protect us from infection and cancer by destroying cells that are recognized as different or foreign," said Christopher M. Walker, PhD, director, Center for Vaccines and Immunity at The Research Institute and one of the study authors. "Parts of the corrected dystrophin protein are clearly foreign because of the patient's DMD gene deletion, and so unwanted T cell immunity targeting the repaired muscle cells was a possibility."

The researchers did detect T cell immunity against foreign segments of the corrected dystrophin protein in one patient with a large DMD gene deletion. However, stronger and faster T cell immunity was detected in a second patient with a much smaller DMD gene deletion.

"Strong, rapid immunity in the second patient with a very small DMD gene deletion was a surprise," said Dr. Walker. "The amount of corrected dystrophin protein that is foreign should also be small, and possibly ignored altogether by the T cells."

Immunity Preceded Treatment

The mystery deepened further when T cell immunity to dystrophin was found to have been present in this patient even before treatment. Careful examination of the muscle revealed that the T cells present before gene therapy recognized dystrophin that is produced in a very small percentage of muscle cells that naturally self-correct the defective DMD gene. Delivery of the gene therapy vector to biceps muscle boosted and accelerated this pre-existing immune response.

New Knowledge About MD

"This study is significant because it documents immunity against a dystrophin protein designed to treat the disease. That may be broadly important to the entire field of gene therapy," said Dr. Mendell. "But it is even more important because of what it might mean for our basic understanding of muscle disease in DMD. We've known for a long time that T cells naturally invade muscles of DMD patients. Drugs that suppress immunity can prolong the time until they are confined to a wheelchair, but we never knew how or why this worked. This gene therapy study has led to the new basic discovery that even small amounts of dystrophin naturally produced

> **FAST FACT**
>
> There are more than eighty types of autoimmune diseases, which are characterized by the body's immune system's mistakenly attacking one of its own organs or systems.

A light micrograph of the muscle protein dystrophin is shown here. Green fluorescent dye highlights the dystrophic layer found in muscle cells. Deficiency in this protein causes muscular dystrophy. (© Patrick Landmann/ Photo Researchers, Inc.)

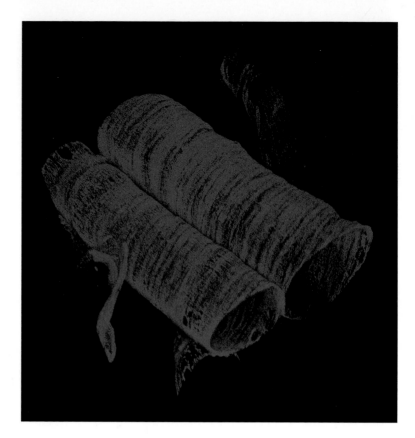

from self-correcting DMD genes can trigger destructive T cells, and they may target muscle cells in a process that resembles autoimmunity."

"The results from this small gene therapy trial underscore the importance of rigorous safety monitoring during all phases of clinical trials, but particularly at the early stages," said neurologist Valerie Cwik, MDA executive vice president for research and medical director. "The wealth of information about the immune system's reaction to gene therapy obtained from this study will aid in design of future clinical trials for DMD and, perhaps, other genetic neuromuscular diseases."

"Many of the on and off switches that regulate T cell immunity in humans are being identified," said Dr. Walker. "We are now attempting to manipulate these switches to enhance T cell immunity in patients with cancer and chronic viral infections. Once we understand the scope and significance of the T cell response against muscle in DMD, it may be possible to harness the same approaches to shut them off. This would move us closer to the goal of slowing muscle loss in DMD and ultimately to prevent immune responses against therapeutic dystrophin protein."

This research was made possible by support from the Muscular Dystrophy Association and Jesse's Journey, and the U.S. Department of Health and Human Services.

Trials Fail to Prove Ataluren as Effective for Treating Muscular Dystrophy

Quest Magazine

The process of getting a drug to market in the United States is highly complex. Pharmaceuticals have to clear three phases of testing before they can be sold to the public. The first phase is designed to establish that the drug is safe. Phase two is designed to demonstrate that the drug is efficacious—in other words, that it works. In the following selection *Quest Magazine* reports that a drug called ataluren has failed its phase two trial. *Quest* reports that the manufacturer has halted the trial after participants failed to benefit sufficiently from the drug therapy to warrant continuing. The trial ran for forty-eight weeks and produced some informative results, but the boys suffering from muscular dystrophy who took the drug were unable on the whole to complete a six-minute walking test that was the benchmark for the drug's success. *Quest Magazine* is a publication of the Muscular Dystrophy Association.

The biopharmaceutical firm PTC Therapeutics announced March 3 [2010] that ataluren, its experimental drug for certain forms of Duchenne (DMD) and Becker (BMD) muscular dystrophy, although safe and well tolerated, failed to meet its primary end point within the 48-week duration of the phase 2b trial. That end point was an improvement in how far boys with DMD or BMD could walk in six minutes.

PTC Therapeutics, which has received $1.75 million in grant funding from MDA [the Muscular Dystrophy Association] for development of ataluren, has partnered with Genzyme Corp. for development of this compound. The experimental drug, which showed promise in preliminary clinical and preclinical trials, was designed to treat cases of DMD and BMD that are the result of flaws called "nonsense mutations" in the dystrophin gene.

Genzyme Corporation partnered with PTC Therapeutics to produce the drug ataluren. Tests of the drug's performance have failed to confirm its effectiveness in treating muscular dystrophy. (© AP Images/Bizuaychu Tesfaye)

Bypassing Bad Genes

Ataluren allows muscle cells to "read through" these nonsense mutations (also called premature stop codons) and produce functional dystrophin protein, a critical component of muscle, which is lacking or reduced in individuals with DMD and BMD. PTC is continuing its analysis of the effect of ataluren on dystrophin levels in trial participants.

"We're extremely disappointed in this result," said Valerie Cwik, MDA Executive Vice President–Research and Medical Director. "But we expect to learn important information from further analysis of the data and, of course, remain steadfast in our commitment to finding effective treatments for Duchenne and Becker dystrophies."

Not a Total Loss

Cwik said that one of the most important questions "is whether raising dystrophin levels in boys with DMD or BMD will restore or preserve function, and if so, how much dystrophin is needed. When all the data from this well-conducted ataluren trial are fully analyzed, we will learn a great deal, which will inform us as we develop other therapies for these diseases."

Langdon Miller, PTC's chief medical officer, echoed these sentiments, saying, "This trial does provide a wealth of valuable data about ataluren and DBMD [DMD/BMD]. Additional analyses will guide the overall clinical and regulatory path forward."

PTC is developing ataluren for cystic fibrosis and hemophilia as well, and these programs are not affected by the DMD/BMD trial result.

Ataluren is an experimental drug that causes cells, such as muscle cells, to "read through," or ignore, premature stop signals in genes, such as in the dystrophin

> **FAST FACT**
>
> The National Institutes of Health surveyed parents of participants in the ataluren study to gain their perspectives on whether the drug had helped.

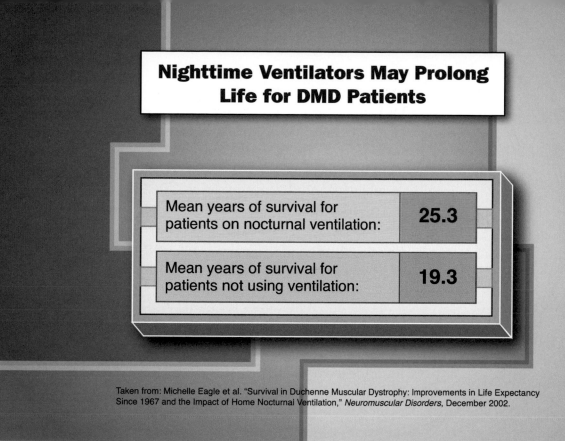

Nighttime Ventilators May Prolong Life for DMD Patients

Mean years of survival for patients on nocturnal ventilation:	25.3
Mean years of survival for patients not using ventilation:	19.3

Taken from: Michelle Eagle et al. "Survival in Duchenne Muscular Dystrophy: Improvements in Life Expectancy Since 1967 and the Impact of Home Nocturnal Ventilation," *Neuromuscular Disorders*, December 2002.

gene. Such premature stop signals cause cells to stop protein synthesis too early, before a functional protein has been made.

Promising Indications

Preliminary results announced in 2007 for ataluren (originally called PTC124) were encouraging. In early studies involving 38 boys with DMD who took PTC124 for about a month, there were indications that muscle destruction had lessened, and dystrophin production increased in at least some trial participants.

The recently completed phase 2b trial lasted 48 weeks and included 174 participants at 37 sites in North America, Europe, Australia and Israel. Participants, all of whom were still walking, were randomly assigned to receive either a low dose of ataluren, a high dose of ataluren, or a placebo.

Various Measures of Success

In addition to the six-minute walk test, which was the primary outcome measure, the investigators evaluated other outcomes, such as participants' activity at home, muscle and heart function, strength, cognitive ability, muscle integrity and dystrophin levels. PTC is currently conducting additional efficacy analyses.

Although the results of this large-scale trial of ataluren were not what the DMD/BMD community had hoped, the knowledge gained from this trial will aid in the design of therapies and future trials.

Development of therapies for DMD/BMD continues. These include:

- gene and cell therapy approaches to replace nonfunctional dystrophin genes with functional dystrophin genes;
- exon skipping, a technology by which cells can create dystrophin protein from a flawed dystrophin gene;
- approaches that could substitute alternate muscle proteins, such as utrophin, for dystrophin; and
- other compounds that target nonsense mutations.

In addition, two cardiac drugs already on the market are being tested in DMD for their ability to protect both heart and skeletal muscle.

Low Doses of Ataluren Did Improve Muscular Dystrophy Symptoms

John Gever

Attempts to develop treatments for muscular dystrophy have generally ended in frustration. Sometimes, though, there are silver linings. In the selection that follows John Gever reports that a research physician contends that the experimental drug ataluren actually performed quite well for muscular dystrophy patients enrolled in a now-halted study. Although the researchers agree that the patients did not achieve the milestone that would have resulted in the trial being declared a success, the physician says that those on a low dose of the drug came very close and that this should not be overlooked. Patients on a high dose regimen did not seem to benefit, explains Gever, though the reasons are obscure. Gever serves as a senior editor of MedPage Today, an online news service for physicians.

SOURCE: John Gever, "ANN: Details of Failed MD Drug Test Disclosed," MedPage Today, April 19, 2010. www.medpagetoday .com. Copyright © 2010 by Everyday Health, Inc. All rights reserved. Reproduced by permission.

An academic researcher said here [in Toronto] that an investigational drug for muscular dystrophy actually did better in a placebo-controlled phase IIb trial than its manufacturer suggested in a press release last month [March 2010].

Patients treated with low-dose ataluren (PTC124), an oral small-molecule agent, had a mean improvement of 29 meters in their six-minute walk distance relative to placebo-treated patients, just short of the 30 meters that was the study's primary efficacy endpoint, according to Brenda L.Y. Wong, MD, of Cincinnati Children's Medical Center, one of the site investigators in the trial.

FAST FACT

In October 2010 PTC Therapeutics announced that trial data indicated that ataluren does indeed slow the loss of walking ability in some muscular dystrophy patients.

A Significant Improvement

Speaking at the the American Academy of Neurology's annual meeting, Wong also said the difference from placebo was statistically significant [using] ranked analysis of covariance, though not with the simple analysis of covariance test that had been prespecified.

When ataluren's manufacturer, PTC Therapeutics, announced trial results last month, it said simply that "the primary endpoint of change in six-minute walk distance did not reach statistical significance within the 48-week duration of the study," giving no other details.

Ataluren forces proper translation of the gene for dystrophin when it contains a nonsense mutation. Such mutations account for about 13% of all cases of Duchenne/Becker muscular dystrophy, Wong said. Other types of mutations, such as deletions, account for the majority of cases, although the end result in all cases is lack of normal dystrophin protein.

Vaulting the Nonsense Mutations

With nonsense mutations, what normally happens during translation is that the ribosome halts when it reaches the garbled code. Ataluren causes the ribosome to skip over the mutation and continue translating the gene, ceasing as it should when it reaches the stop codon.

The trial randomized 174 patients to placebo or one of two doses of ataluren for 48 weeks. The mean baseline score in six-minute walk distance was about 360 meters.

The low dose consisted of 10 mg/kg [10 milligrams of drug for every kilogram of a patient's body weight] in the morning, 10 mg/kg at midday, and 20 mg/kg in the evening. Each of these was doubled in the high-dose group.

An unexpected result was that the high-dose group was no more effective than placebo: both of these groups recorded a 42-meter reduction in six-minute walk distance over the 48-week study.

Less Is More?

The low-dose group, however, had a reduction of only 13 meters.

The low-dose regimen was also significantly better than either placebo or the high dose in the median time [it took a patient] to [attain a] 10% worsening in six-minute walk distance.

Wong said the investigators were now trying to figure out why the high dose was so much less effective than the

Ataluren, an experimental drug developed by PTC Therapeutics for muscular dystrophy patients, was intended to force proper translation of the gene for dystrophin when it contains a nonsense mutation. (© AP Images/PRNewsFoto/ PTC Therapeutics)

The United States Has the Third-Highest Estimated Number of New Muscular Dystrophy Cases Annually

Taken from: Wrong Diagnosis, "Statistics by Country for Muscular Dystrophy: Incidence of Muscular Dystrophy," www.wrongdiagnosis.com.

lower dose. One possibility, she said, was that it affects ribosomal activity too strongly, so that the resulting protein ends up malformed.

Investigators collected muscle biopsies during the study to measure dystrophin levels, but the results had not been analyzed yet, she said.

PTC and its development partner, Genzyme, are also testing the drug in other genetic disorders caused by nonsense mutations, including cystic fibrosis and hemophilia A and B.

PERSPECTIVES ON DISEASES AND DISORDERS

White Muscular Dystrophy Patients Live Longer than Blacks with MD

Madison Park

Disparities in disease are nothing new; however, it is especially poignant to learn that advances in treating muscular dystrophy have left some groups of people behind. In the following selection Madison Park, contributing to Sanjay Gupta's blog on CNN.com, reports that African Americans have not benefited nearly as much as white Americans from progress in muscular dystrophy treatments. White male muscular dystrophy patients in particular have far outstripped black male patients in longevity gains, and muscular dystrophy strikes many more men than women. Researchers are not sure why there is so much disparity along racial lines. Park is a writer and producer for CNNhealth.com.

Whites with muscular dystrophy live up to 12 years longer than their African American counterparts, according to a study published in [the September 2010 issue of] *Neurology*.

SOURCE: Madison Park, "Study: Whites with Muscular Dystrophy Live Up to 12 Years Longer than Blacks," CNNHealth.com, September 13, 2010. Courtesy, CNN.

Although medical advancements over a period of 20 years [have] increased the life span of patients with the debilitating muscle disease, those improvements haven't been equal among different groups. White women with muscular dystrophy had a median death age of 63, versus 51 for African American women. For men, their median age at death was 33, versus 23 for African American males.

Muscular dystrophy is a group of inherited muscle diseases in which the muscle fibers are unusually susceptible to damage and progressively weaken. The condition can lead to early death due to respiratory or heart failure.

Men More Often Fall Victim

Men tend to die younger, because the vast majority of patients who die have Duchenne muscular dystrophy—a particular type of the disorder that rarely affects females.

Researchers from the Centers for Disease Control and Prevention and University of Pennsylvania set out to identify trends in muscular dystrophy between 1985 to 2005 and analyzed 18,315 death certificates associated with the disease in the United States.

Over this study period, both groups saw improvements in lifespan because of better lung care and other therapies, said one of the study authors, Dr. Richard Finkel.

"For white males overall, there was a 22-year increase in the age at death (from about 22 to 44 years) while for blacks the increase was only about 6.6 years," said Finkel, clinical professor of Neurology at University of Pennsylvania school of medicine and director of the Neuromuscular Program at the Children's Hospital Philadelphia. "So both groups improved but not to the same extent."

FAST FACT

African Americans suffer worse outcomes than white Americans in numerous diseases, including cancer, stroke, and HIV/AIDS.

Reasons for Disparity Are Elusive

This racial disparity could be due to sociocultural barriers, genetic factors or other factors, but it's impossible to pinpoint the reasons based on death certificates, Finkel said.

"There's no way we can get beneath the surface and find out whether there are socio-economic factors that play a role," Finkel said. "Are there genetic factors in blacks versus whites that may play a role? Are there other factors in blacks that compound the problem? This study tried to take that into account—but that's not the entire answer."

Another finding was that cardiomyopathy, which is weakening of the heart muscle or a change in heart muscle structure, was more often reported in black men (20.9 percent) than white men (11.8 percent).

Researchers have found that white male muscular dystrophy patients live as much as twelve years longer than African American patients. Scientists have yet to discover the reasons for this disparity. (© **AP Images/M. Spencer Green**)

Why Duchenne and Becker MD Strike Boys Almost Exclusively

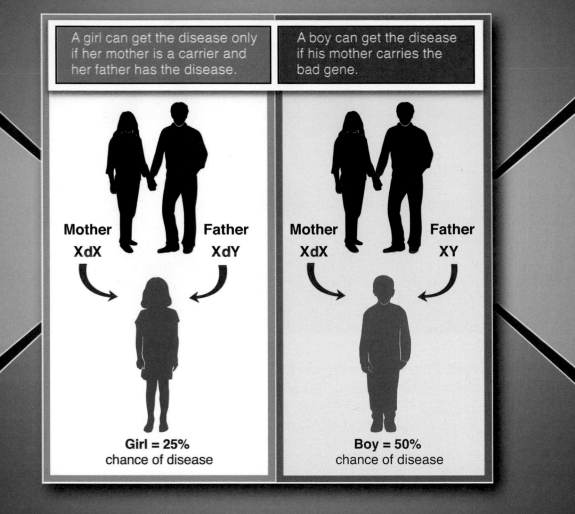

A girl can get the disease only if her mother is a carrier and her father has the disease.

A boy can get the disease if his mother carries the bad gene.

Mother
XdX

Father
XdY

Mother
XdX

Father
XY

Girl = 25%
chance of disease

Boy = 50%
chance of disease

Taken from: Molly E. Rideout, "Muscular Dystrophies: Excerpt from *The 5-Minute Pediatric Consult*," Wrong Diagnosis, 2008. www.wrongdiagnosis.com.

The authors cautioned in the study that "this dataset did not include information about quality of life, so increases in age at death do not necessarily equate with improvements in quality of life."

CHAPTER 3

Personal Narratives

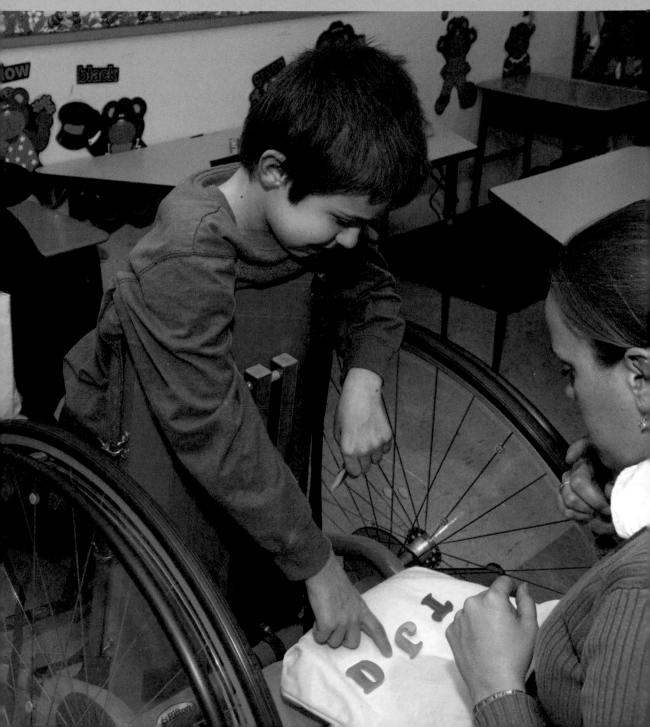

A Woman with a Rare Form of Muscular Dystrophy Talks About Living with the Disease

Mandy Van Benthuysen

Muscular dystrophy is an incurable and debilitating disease. But while it may waste muscles, the following selection shows that it cannot touch the human spirit. Mandy Van Benthuysen describes her life with limb-girdle muscular dystrophy (LGMD). She was four when she was diagnosed. The news came like a thunderbolt to her family; however, her parents steadied themselves and educated themselves about how to manage the disease. Van Benthuysen had to get leg braces early on and eventually needed a wheelchair and other equipment. But with the support of her family and the Muscular Dystrophy Association (MDA), which published her story, she persevered. She became the MDA's national youth chairperson, graduated from college, and found work in the television industry. Following her graduation from Arizona State University, Van Benthuysen became a production assistant on the *Dr. Phil* show. She later moved to a job with TVTracker.com, a Hollywood-based firm.

Photo on previous page. A ten-year-old boy with Duchenne muscular dystrophy (DMD) works with a therapist. Most boys who have DMD die at around age twenty. (© Ellen B. Senisi/Photo Researchers, Inc.)

SOURCE: Mandy Van Benthuysen, "Facts About Limb-Girdle Muscular Dystrophies," Muscular Dystrophy Association, April 2010. All rights reserved. Reproduced by permission.

When I was 4 years old, my parents took me to a specialist to find out why I walked with an unusual waddle. They learned I had limb-girdle muscular dystrophy [LGMD].

Like many of you, we were shocked and scared by this diagnosis. My parents wondered why I had this disease; we had no history of it in our family. But . . . LGMD is caused by any of several rare genetic defects that people may not even know they have. That means it wasn't caused by anything you or your parents did, and you didn't catch it from anyone.

From Leg Braces to a Scooter

My family had to learn a lot about muscular dystrophy and make some major adjustments, both physical and psychological. Our world came to include doctor visits, leg braces, physical therapy and lots of questions. But gradually, muscular dystrophy just became a part of our lives, and we coped with it by learning all we could. Thanks to my determined parents, my devoted sister and the help of the Muscular Dystrophy Association [MDA], I had a wonderful childhood.

> **FAST FACT**
>
> The Muscular Dystrophy Association is best known for its former national chairman and telethon host, iconic comedian Jerry Lewis.

I graduated from college, and I'm now working in L.A. [Los Angeles] in the television industry. I use a wheelchair or scooter part time to help me when I work, travel and have fun with my friends.

I hope you can tell from my story that having limb-girdle muscular dystrophy doesn't mean the end of your choices or your dreams. It isn't easy to live with muscles that grow weaker over time, but you can have a very rewarding life with this condition.

Overcoming Disability

Not everyone with LGMD has the same experience, but most of those I've met have busy, fulfilling lives like mine.

$61,013,855

Jerry Lewis (pictured) hosted the Muscular Dystrophy Association's telethon for forty-five years, raising billions of dollars to fight the disease. The author served for six years as the MDA's national youth chairperson. (© AP Images/Jane Kalinowsky)

I know of a writer, a doctor, an air traffic controller, some teachers, school and college administrators, a real estate professional, a travel agency operator—all with limb-girdle MD. Many of these bright, active, independent people are married, and some have children—and grandchildren.

Those of us with LGMD have a lot of support today. People with disabilities have more opportunities than ever before to develop and use their abilities. Federal law guarantees us a public education, equal employment opportunity and access to public places. Computers and technology help me and other people with muscular dystrophy to move around, write, work and drive.

By far, my greatest ally in living with LGMD is MDA; I'm sure my parents would say the same thing. . . . The Association is also the world leader in research on neuromuscular diseases, and its scientists have made many exciting discoveries about LGMD in the years since my diagnosis. We all pray for the day when no one has to have a neuromuscular disease.

PERSPECTIVES ON DISEASES AND DISORDERS

An American Muscular Dystrophy Patient Goes to China for Stem Cell Treatment

Russ Kleve

Muscular dystrophy results from faulty genes that lead to loss of muscle cells. It is widely hoped that stem cell therapy will prove successful in treating the disease. Embryonic stem cells are undifferentiated cells that are capable of turning into any type of cell, including muscle cells; however, such treatment has not been approved for humans in the United States. In the selection that follows muscular dystrophy patient Russ Kleve describes his journey to China in search of better health through stem cell therapy. In an account made up from blog entries, Kleve tells how he traveled all the way to Hangzhou to undergo the treatment. Undergoing stem cell treatment was no easy thing. Shortly after his arrival, he learned that his brother, who also suffered from muscular dystrophy, had died. Unable to return without abandoning his treatment, Kleve remained in China. After receiving several rounds of stem cell injections into his muscles, he described himself as a human pincushion. Nevertheless, for all the suffering he endured, he believes the treatments did him good. Kleve is a senior paralegal at a law firm in Portland, Oregon.

March 11, 2009. I, along with my mother, twin sister, one older and one younger brothers, were all born with Facioscapulohumeral muscular dystrophy ("FSHD" for short). The major symptom of FSHD is the progressive weakening and loss of skeletal muscles. The usual location of these weaknesses at onset is the origin of the name: face (facio), shoulder girdle (scapulo) and upper arms (humeral). Early weaknesses of the muscles of the eye (open and close) and mouth (smile, pucker, whistle) are distinctive for FSHD.

Unlike my siblings, my disability did not really begin to [affect] me until my late-20's, when my left foot began to turn inward causing me to trip. This is known as footdrop. Prior to this I was an avid bicyclist, cranking out 50–100 miles a week, rain or shine. However, by the time I was 30 I had traded my touring bike for a stationary bike; by 35 even that was difficult to pedal; by 40 I had given it up altogether. Now, at 48 . . . life's simple movements are a struggle, although I consider myself extremely lucky when I think about my own family members and what they must deal with every day.

I dedicate this journey to my brother, Scott, severely affected by FSHD in his childhood who passed away in 1995, too young at 38; to my mother who left us in 2002 at the age of 72; my sister Teresa, and my brother Craig, everyone who lives with this disability and those who support and love them. . . .

The Chosen Method of Treatment

Stem cells are derived from a single umbilical cord provided by a full-term, live birth, Chinese baby (local is fresher!). My specific program will include six injections (10–15 million stem cells each) into my lower spine, as well as a bone marrow treatment which requires the insertion of a long needle into my hip. The marrow is extracted, cultivated and a nerve growth factor is added. Nerve growth factor is taken from the cord serum, and its purpose is to encourage the growth and repair of neurons as well as enhancing the potential of the umbilical stem cells. The bone marrow is then reinjected via the lumbar [vertebrae]. But wait, there's more poking! I'll be hooked up to an IV [intravenous] drip containing stem cells, and site injections of stem cells into specific muscle groups will also be part of the treatment. I understand that six days a week I'll be going to some sort of physical therapy, physiotherapy, acupuncture and massage, along with traditional Chinese herbal therapy. . . .

March 15, 2009. Nearly 25 hours, and four airports later we're here! I'm traveling with my girlfriend Laurie's son-in-law, Jason, who has been a great help getting me out of wheelchairs and airplane seats, fetching liquids to quench pressurized cabin thirst and snacks between stops. Beike Biotech [the company that organized the treatment] requires you bring a caregiver or hire one once you get here [China]. I'm glad I brought someone I know and can trust. There's no way I could have made it here otherwise. The flights were uneventful—just the way you want them.

> **FAST FACT**
>
> Researchers in Italy have shown that genetically corrected cells from mice with muscular dystrophy can build stronger muscles when injected back into the mice.

Everything was on time and with too much turbulence. Air China was cramped for the 13 hour leg, but our row-mate Peter, made it interesting. Peter originated from Taiwan, and eventually made his way to California, where he and his family sucessfully embraced the American Way, himself eventually becoming an American citizen. Peter works in the luxury car import/export [business], and was making yet another trip to China. He told us how to make friends in China by passing out cigarettes to the men and beauty products for the women.

Tragic News from Home

March 17, 2009. It is with a heavy heart I type this post today. I learned that my brother Craig died while we were in flight this past Sunday. Craig was 47, and had dealt with the ravages of muscular dystrophy since he was very young. Of us four kids, his case was second in severity. In late February he came down with a severe case of pneumonia. If not for the insistence of his wonderful care provider, Jay Graham, he would never have made it that far. After nine days in ICU [the intensive care unit], the doctors were able to replace his ventilator with a breathing tube and he spoke freely, exclaiming, "tell everyone I'm alive!" But even though the fluid was off his lung, the damage, coupled with a weakened body, was already done. He eventually was moved out of ICU, where I got a good two hours' talk [with him] before I left for China. He was smiling and happy to hear he was going home the next day. I will miss my brother, and wish him health and happiness now that he has gone to be with Mom and Scott. Take care, Buddy, and watch over me will ya?

The Treatment Begins

March 18, 2009. The first stem cell packet [was] given to me on March 18 via IV. The most immediate sensation was very twitchy legs, like I had energy to spare. Jason and I had to take a walk around the ward about 3 hours after the treatment. My legs twitched most of the night, but I finally got some sleep.

This morning, my gait was noticeably faster, and I was looking forward to the two hour daily physical therapy with "No Mercy James," my 26-year-old therapist. My protocol has changed a bit. The doctors say for muscular dystrophy patients, lumbar injections will not work as well as site injections into the muscle groups. They have not told me yet when the site injections will begin, but the IVs of stem cells will be weekly. Also, for about 40 minutes each day I have acupuncture treatment. The Chinese use a needle about twice the length and girth of US needles for this. They push them into the muscle then hook them up to an electrical stimulator. Yeah, I know,

A Thai doctor prepares stem cells for injection into a patient. Author Russ Kleve went to China for the same stem cell procedure, because it has not been approved in the United States.
(© Agnes Dherbeys/VII Mentor Program/Corbis)

sounds painful, and it is, a little, but that's the cost, so I'll pay it. After acupuncture they hook me up for another 40 minutes to a TENS [transcutaneous electrical nerve stimulation] machine and send electrical current through my legs and arms stimulating the muscles again, but there are no needles involved. It's actually relaxing.

Next Tuesday will be the bone marrow extraction. I'll be completely put under for this procedure. The next day will be another IV of stem cells. . . .

Round Three

March 30, 2009. I've been under the weather with a slight cold accompanied with a sore throat for the past four days now. This is not the best circumstances for baby stem cells to develop so they've had me on traditional Chinese medicines which includes a small vial of some pretty "vile" tasting liquid four times a day, as well as some sort of pills. I have no idea what's in either of these products, but they seem to be helping. Jason was able to round up some vitamin C so I've added that to the mix too.

Today I was given my third bag of stem cells via IV. On Friday they will return my cultivated bone marrow via IV. Then next Wednesday, I'll be put under general anesthesia and given two bags of stem cells via site injections into my thighs, calfs, forearms and biceps. This will complete all the transfusions I've signed up for. After that it's workout, workout, workout. I expect to increase my physical therapy from two to three hours a day.

Results: So far not much at all, except maybe a slightly faster walking gait. But I've only just now had my third (of six) treatment, and it's way too soon to tell. One of the Americans who works here told me muscle damage takes longer than other types of treatment to see results because you have to work and develop the muscles. But the new building blocks will be in place by the time I leave here, so the rest will be up to me. Cool! Bring it on!! . . .

The Final Treatment

April 17, 2009. This afternoon was my final round of intramuscular injections using two bags of umbilical cord stem cells. I received 40 injections into the front and back of my legs; 24 in my thighs and 16 in my calves. Altogether, eight bags of stem cells have now been used, along with one bone marrow treatment using my own stem cells, cultivated with a specialized growth factor. Now the real work begins with daily exercise and physical therapy in order to build new muscle over the next several months. . . .

April 19, 2009. Excellent News! This morning the nurses took a few vials of my blood to check my levels. I learned this afternoon that everything was "normal." I then asked specifically about my CK level. CK is short for Creatine Kinase, which is a type of protein called an enzyme. It catalyzes or "encourages" a biochemical reaction to occur. The normal function of CK in our cells is to add a phosphate group to creatine, turning it into the high-energy molecule phosphocreatine, which is burned as a quick source of energy by our cells.

During the process of muscle degeneration, as in FSH muscular dystrophy patients, muscle cells break open and find their way into the blood stream. Because most of the CK in the body normally exists in muscle, a rise in the amount of CK in the blood indicates that muscle damage has occurred or is occurring. In healthy adults, the CK levels can vary depending on gender, race and activity, but normal range is 22 to 198.

Arguably, CK is not a definitive measure of the progression of any muscular disorder, but in my case I have monitored it for the past 10+ years based on my doctor's tests. . . . When I arrived in China in mid-March for my treatment, my CK was 188, a drop from 209 in November of '08. Now it's at 74, which may indicate the progression of my disease has slowed down or stopped altogether! . . .

Returning Home

April 23, 2009. After a 25 hour trip, Jason and I returned to Oregon from our five week trip to Hangzhou, China, on April 21. While we were having our first real US meal on a layover in San Francisco, we saw [actor] Dustin Hoffman walk by in front of us!

Anyway, it's nice to be home. Thank you Beike Biotech for all your wonderful care and treatment!

Now it's time to get to work and continue my physical therapy. . . .

Benefits Recede over Time

June 29, 2010. Well, I guess it's time to say goodbye and wrap up this little blog. It has been 14 months since I returned from China from umbilical cord stem cell treatment. As I mentioned before, my results at first were significant but seem to have leveled off within six or eight months of my return.

Everyone will experience their own results from stem cell treatment. I hope yours is awesome—I guarantee it will be life-changing.

I want to thank all 2,456 of you that have continued to read my blog, followed up with questions and traveled with me on this journey. Your support has been invaluable.

Life Without a Smile

Sarabjit Parmar

In so many ways, life with muscular dystrophy can be grim. For Sarabjit Parmar of Great Britain, there is a cruel twist to her disease: It has robbed her of the ability to smile. In the selection that follows she tells of the devastating implications of that disability. To be unable to smile is to give an impression of being a coldhearted, unfeeling, callous person. As readers soon learn, Parmar is certainly not cold hearted, but she suffers from facioscapulohumeral muscular dystrophy—known as FSHD for short. FSHD affects the whole body, but it first attacks the muscles of the face. That's why Parmar has been unable to smile for as long as she can remember. The result is that people recoil in fear or disgust—even little children. Fortunately, her family and those who get to know her come to understand how she's feeling through other means. More fortunately still, Parmar is strong enough and self-aware enough to cope with the social distress of being unable to smile. Parmar is a writer from Leicester, England. She graduated with a degree in communications from the University of Derby in early 2011.

SOURCE: Sarabjit Parmar, "If Someone Smiles, All I Can Do Is Look the Other Way, Embarrassed That I Can't Return the Gesture," *Guardian*, May 29, 2009. Copyright © Guardian News & Media Ltd 2009. Reproduced by permission.

From the day I was born I have never smiled. As a child I don't think I ever questioned it. It sounds bizarre, but I never acknowledged that it was a physical impossibility. The first time the seriousness of it really hit me was when I was in my teens. People would look at me and say, "Smile! It may never happen!" Photographers would call out, "Smile!" I'd sigh, roll my eyes and feel humiliated.

My parents, of course, noticed much earlier. When I was a young child, they took me to a doctor but were told I was probably a late developer. When nothing changed, they took me back. From that moment, I was constantly visiting hospitals and consultants, being prodded and examined. But it wasn't until I was 10 that I was finally diagnosed with FSHD—facioscapulohumeral muscular dystrophy. This rare genetic condition affects the muscles in the face, shoulders and upper arms. It causes a progressive weakening of skeletal muscles. Some may find their bodies are weakened: others, such as me, face harsher circumstances.

When I was 12, I started to limp and was constantly out of breath. By 14, it took all my strength even to lift a foot. My spine developed a curve and I became a permanent wheelchair-user. That was the worst moment of my life; it felt as if one minute I was a happy, carefree girl who could do whatever I wanted and the next I was confined to a piece of metal. I closed off from the world and felt totally lost.

Learning Tough Lessons

Yet my disability taught me not to take anything for granted. I had to toughen up and learn to laugh when people looked down on me. And although, for a long time, I thought I would never be independent, I have discovered I can do anything I want to. One thing I will never do, however, is smile.

People's smiles are often the first thing I notice. I think of Mother Teresa's quote, "We shall never know all the good that a simple smile can do", and realise that it's true. I know a smile can light someone's day and break the ice.

Although it seems like a small thing, there are times when it can be really distressing. One day, I was happily clothes shopping with a friend, as usual admiring the shoe section. As I tried on a pair of gorgeous hot-pink high heels a cute, blond-haired little boy came to stand by my wheelchair. He was no more than two or three years old and as he gazed up at me he fiddled nervously with the action-man figure in his hands. I looked away, thinking, "Bless him." When after a minute or two I noticed that he was still there, I glanced at him again. Unexpectedly his face broke into a shy smile. The look on his face and his blue eyes willed me to smile back. And at that moment, I wished more than ever that I could return it. When I couldn't, I felt terrible. He looked back at my unmoving face so upset, scared and con-fused and I just didn't know what to do. His mother came to pull him away, shooting me a disgusted look. And I felt the familiar emotion I felt as a child, the one that's persistently nudging me, tell-ing me that I'm different and will never entirely belong.

> **FAST FACT**
>
> According to the Facioscapulohumeral Muscular Dystrophy Society, an added cruelty of FSHD is that the muscle atrophy and loss of function occur asymmetrically, so that, for example, lips twist and one side of the back hunches.

Fear of First Encounters

It is frustrating to think that people might be left with a bad impression of me because my face looks cold and aloof. I must admit, when meeting someone new, the first thought that pops into my head is, "Here we go again; I've got to explain the whole palaver." The fear of how I will be perceived makes me anxious, and I worry that people will treat me differently. I know I must say something. But if someone on the street smiles, all I can do is look the other way, embarrassed by not being able to return the gesture and not being able to explain.

My friends and family can tell by the tone of my voice if I am happy, and if I find something funny, I laugh out loud. And I have learned to poke fun at myself, even using my facial paralysis to tease my friends. If I'm unusually quiet and a friend says, "You look upset, what's up?" I'll retort, "What do you want me to do? Smile?"

Now, if someone gave me the chance to smile I wouldn't take it. I've learned to live without it and my disability has made me strong-willed and determined. It has also taught me to think twice before judging others. It shouldn't matter whether you can't smile, or you have three legs or a purple face. What matters is that everyone feels integrated.

GLOSSARY

amino acids The units from which a protein is built. The sequence of amino acids determines the shape, properties, and role of a protein.

animal models A term used by researchers for experiments performed on animals (usually mice or rats) to study how certain therapies might affect humans.

atrophy A wasting away of tissue, such as muscle.

autosomal A condition that affects males and females equally.

Becker muscular dystrophy (BMD) A type of disorder similar to Duchenne muscular dystrophy but less severe. Like Duchenne, it is caused by a genetic flaw that results in a lack of the dystrophin protein.

carrier A bearer and transmitter of a disease-causing gene.

carrier testing Genetic testing to find out whether a person with no symptoms of a condition possesses a faulty gene that could be transmitted to offspring.

creatine kinase A kind of protein found in muscle that serves as a marker for MD. Certain muscular dystrophies are associated with high levels of creatine kinase in the blood.

DNA Deoxyribonucleic acid, the long molecule that contains a person's genome. Mutations in the sequence of DNA can lead to genetic diseases such as MD.

dominant pattern of inheritance A kind of genetic transmission in which a single abnormal copy of a gene causes disease, even though a good copy of the gene is also present.

Duchenne muscular dystrophy (DMD)	The most widespread variety of the genetic disorder in which muscle cells break down and eventually die, causing muscle wasting. It generally affects only males.
dystrophin	The essential protein missing from those who have Duchenne muscular dystrophy and nearly absent in those who have Becker muscular dystrophy. Dystrophin normally protects muscle fibers during contraction.
facioscapulohumeral muscular dystrophy (FSHD)	A variety of MD characterized by the muscles it first attacks; namely, in the face, shoulder blades, and upper arms.
gene therapy	The treatment of a genetic disease by the introduction of a replacement gene into a cell through a virus or other means.
genes	Segments of DNA that contain the set of instructions for the production of a specific protein. Genes usually come in pairs, one inherited from each parent. A mutation in a gene can lead to a disease, unless the partner gene in a pair is dominant.
genetic disorders	Conditions that result from alterations in genes.
genome	The complete set of genes of a person or organism.
limb-girdle muscular dystrophy (LGMD)	A variety of MD that is characterized by its primarily attacking the muscles around the shoulders and hips.
mutation	An alteration in a gene from its original state. Mutations occur spontaneously or result from environmental factors such as radiation. Mutations in the reproductive cells, known as gametes (sperm and egg), are inherited by offspring.
myopathy	A disease condition affecting muscle, usually without involvement of the nerves.
protein	Proteins are formed from linked amino acids and serve as the basic building blocks of cells.

sex chromosomes The X and Y chromosomes determine the sex of an individual. Two X chromosomes make a female; an X and Y chromosome make a male.

translational research The application of knowledge gained from scientific medical research in the laboratory to studies in humans.

utrophin Short for "ubiquitous dystrophin," it is a protein similar to dystrophin that some researchers believe may be able to substitute for missing dystrophin in MD patients.

vector A vehicle, usually a virus, for transferring genetic material into a cell during gene therapy.

X-linked A gene that appears on the X chromosome, making boys susceptible to a single defective copy. (Boys have only one X chromosome, from their mothers, along with a Y chromosome from their fathers.)

CHRONOLOGY

1836   Italian medical professor Gaetano Conte records an unknown disease, later identified as Duchenne muscular dystrophy.

circa 1860   French neurology pioneer Guillaume Duchenne de Boulogne describes the characteristics of the disease that comes to be named for him: Duchenne muscular dystrophy.

1884   French physicians Louis Landouzy and Joseph Dejerine first describe facioscapulohumeral muscular dystrophy (FSHD).

1891   German neurologist Wilhelm Heinrich Erb introduces the term "progressive muscular dystrophy" to describe a set of hereditary degenerative diseases.

1930   A new type of MD, sclerotic muscular dystrophy, or Ullrich's dystrophy, is diagnosed.

1950   The Muscular Dystrophy Association is founded.

1951   The term *limb-girdle muscular dystrophy* is introduced.

1953   The first edition of a landmark book titled *Diseases of Muscle*, by Raymond D. Adams, D. Denny-Brown, and Carl M. Pearson, is published.

1957   Peter Emil Becker, a German neurological researcher, publishes a study of the genetics of the second-most common type of muscular dystrophy, since named after him.

1971   British neurologist Sir John Walton compiles a book with many contributors that brings together all that is known about muscular dystrophy and related diseases. *Disorders of Voluntary Muscle* leads many primary care physicians to offer better care to MD patients.

1987   Dr. Ronald Worton at the Hospital for Sick Children in Toronto and Dr. Lou Kunkel at Boston Children's Hospital independently discover the gene defect that causes Duchenne muscular dystrophy.

2000   Congress passes the Children's Health Act, which includes a provision for more intense research into Duchenne muscular dystrophy.

2010   Researchers announce the first success in the use of experimental gene therapy to treat muscular dystrophy.

ORGANIZATIONS TO CONTACT

The editors have compiled the following list of organizations concerned with the issues debated in this book. The descriptions are derived from materials provided by the organizations. All have publications or information available for interested readers. The list was compiled on the date of publication of the present volume; the information provided here may change. Be aware that many organizations take several weeks or longer to respond to inquiries, so allow as much time as possible.

Centers for Disease Control and Prevention (CDC)
1600 Clifton Rd.
Atlanta, GA 30333
(800) CDC-INFO
fax: (770) 488-4760
e-mail: cdcinfo@cdc
.gov
website: www.cdc.gov

The CDC is the nation's leader in efforts to prevent and control diseases, including genetic disorders. Its website has information on muscular dystrophy and research into possible avenues for treatments and cures.

Facioscapulohumeral Muscular Dystrophy (FSH) Society
64 Grove St.
Watertown, MA 02472
(781) 275-7781
(617) 658-7878
fax: (781) 860-0599
e-mail: info@fshsoci
ety.org
website: www.fshsoci
ety.org

The FSH Society bills itself as the world's largest and most progressive grassroots network of facioscapulohumeral muscular dystrophy (FSHD) patients, their families, and research activists. The organization is dedicated to treating and curing FSHD through research and advocating for patients.

Mayo Clinic
200 First St. SW
Rochester, MN 55905
(507) 284-2511
fax: (507) 284-0161
e-mail through
website: www.mayo
clinic.org

The famed Mayo Clinic, based in Rochester, Minnesota, is a not-for-profit medical center that diagnoses and treats complex medical problems in every specialty, including genetic diseases such as muscular dystrophy. Its staff is known not only for excellence in treatment but also for groundbreaking research.

Muscular Dystrophy Association (MDA)
3300 E. Sunrise Dr.
Tucson, AZ 85718-3208
(520) 529-2000
toll-free: (800) 572-1717
fax: (520) 529-5300
e-mail: mda@mdausa
.org
website: www.mda.org

Best known for its national chairman, Jerry Lewis, and the annual Labor Day telethon he conducted from 1966 through 2011, the MDA is a nonprofit organization dedicated to curing muscular dystrophy, amyotrophic lateral sclerosis, and related neuromuscular diseases by funding worldwide research. The MDA also provides comprehensive health care and support services, advocacy, and education.

Muscular Dystrophy Family Foundation
7220 US 31 South
Indianapolis, IN
46227
(317) 923-6333; toll-free: (800) 544-1213
fax: (317) 923-6334
e-mail: mdff@mdff.org
website: www.mdff.org

The Muscular Dystrophy Family Foundation, also known as the No Boundaries Family Foundation, provides resources, services, and adaptive equipment to enable patients with muscular dystrophy and their family members to live independent and productive lives. In addition to advocacy and education, the foundation provides adaptive equipment and emotional support to individuals and families affected by various neuromuscular diseases.

Myotonic Dystrophy Foundation (MDF)
10016 Foothills Blvd. Ste. 130
Roseville, CA 95747
(916) 788-2626
toll-free: (866) 968-6642
fax: (916) 788-2646
e-mail: info@myo tonic.org
website: www.myo tonic.org

The MDF works to lead and mobilize resources for effective management, treatment, and eventually a cure for myotonic dystrophy. It provides education for affected individuals, their families, medical professionals, and the public; conducts advocacy; and raises funds in the private sector to accelerate understanding of the disease through research.

National Institute of Arthritis and Musculoskeletal and Skin Diseases (NIAMS)
National Institutes of Health
31 Center Dr., Rm. 4C02 MSC 2350
Bethesda, MD 20892-2350
(301) 496-8190
toll-free: (877) 22-NIA MS (226-4267)
e-mail: niamsinfo@mail .nih.gov
website: www.niams.nih .gov

A unit of the National Institutes of Health, NIAMS works to support research into the causes, treatment, and prevention of arthritis and musculoskeletal and skin diseases. This institute also oversees the training of basic and clinical scientists to carry out this research and the dissemination of information on research progress in these diseases, including muscular dystrophy.

National Institute of Child Health and Human Development (NICHD)
National Institutes of Health
31 Center Dr., Rm. 2A32 MSC 2425
Bethesda, MD 20892-2425
(301) 496-5133
website: www.nichd .nih.gov

Part of the National Institutes of Health, the NICHD was established to investigate the general trend of human development as a means of understanding disabilities, including intellectual and developmental disabilities, and the events that occur during pregnancy. Today, the institute conducts and supports research on all stages of human development from preconception to adulthood, including genetic diseases such as muscular dystrophy, that interfere with normal development.

Parent Project Muscular Dystrophy (PPMD)
158 Linwood Plaza
Ste. 220
Fort Lee, NJ 07024
(201) 944-9985; toll-free: (800) 714-KIDS (5437)
fax: (201) 944-9987
e-mail: info@parent projectmd.org
website: www.parent projectmd.org

The PPMD is a nonprofit organization focused entirely on Duchenne muscular dystrophy, the most prevalent form of the disease. The organization takes a comprehensive approach in the fight against Duchenne—funding research, raising awareness, promoting advocacy, connecting the community, and broadening treatment options.

World Health Organization (WHO)
Avenue Appia 20
1211 Geneva 27
Switzerland
+41 22 791 21 11
fax: +41 22 791 31 11
e-mail: info@who.int
website: www.who.int

The WHO is the directing and coordinating authority for health within the United Nations system. It is responsible for providing leadership on global health matters, shaping the health research agenda, setting norms and standards, articulating evidence-based policy options, providing technical support to countries, and monitoring and assessing health trends.

FOR FURTHER READING

Books

Jeffrey S. Chamberlain and Thomas A. Rando, *Duchenne Muscular Dystrophy: Advances in Therapeutics*. New York: Taylor & Francis, 2006.

Alan E.H. Emery, *Muscular Dystrophy (the Facts)*. New York: Oxford University Press, 2008.

Alan E.H. Emery and Marcia L.H. Emery, *The History of a Genetic Disease: Duchenne Muscular Dystrophy or Meryon's Disease*. Oxford: Oxford University Press, 2011.

Lori Laws, *A Blessing in the Storm: Muscular Dystrophy Messed Up My Life and Made Me Whole*. Raleigh, NC: Lulu.com, 2009.

Sally Mann, *Proud Flesh*. New York: Aperture Foundation Books, 2009.

Philip M. Parker, *Emery-Dreifuss Muscular Dystrophy: A Bibliography and Dictionary for Physicians, Patients, and Genome Researchers*. San Diego, CA: Icon Group International, 2007.

Joyce Brennfleck Shannon, ed., *The Muscular Dystrophy Sourcebook*. Detroit: Omnigraphics, 2004.

Irwin M. Siegel, *Muscular Dystrophy in Children: A Guide for Families*. New York: Demos, 1999.

Kate Stone, Claire Tester, Joy Blakeney, and Alex Howarth, *Occupational Therapy and Duchenne Muscular Dystrophy*. West Sussex, UK: John Wiley, 2007.

Penny Wolfson, *Moonrise: One Family, Genetic Identity, and Muscular Dystrophy*. New York: St. Martin's, 2003.

Periodicals and Internet Sources

Alison Abbott, "Muscular Dystrophy Findings Fuel French Stem Cell Debate," *NatureNews*, March 31, 2011. www.nature.com/news/2011/110331/full/news.2011.197.html.

Reed Abelson, "Lacking Cure, a New Tack on a Muscle Disease," *New York Times*, February 20, 2008. www.nytimes.com /2008/02/20/business/20dystrophy.html.

Bill Barol, "I Stayed Up with Jerry," *Newsweek*, September 21, 1987. www.newsweek.com/1987/09/21/i-stayed-up-with-jerry .html.

Steve Bornfeld, "Karen Wheeler Doesn't Let Muscular Dystrophy Curtail Her Artistry," *Las Vegas Review Journal*, March 31, 2011. www.lvrj.com/neon/karen-wheeler-doesn-t-let-muscular -dystrophy-curtail-her-artistry-118975179.html.

Jim Brown, "Muscular Dystrophy Association Awards $1.5 Million Grant to Acceleron to Support ACE-031," MedicalNews Today.com, January 8, 2011. www. medicalnewstoday.com /articles/213057.php.

Children's Hospital Boston, "Drug Screen Points the Way to Potential New Duchenne Muscular Dystrophy Treatments," MedicalNewsToday.com, March 19, 2011. www.medicalnews today.com/articles/219635.php.

Sarah Sturmon Dale, "Disabled Enough?," *Time*, April 11, 2005. www.time.com/time/magazine/article/0,9171,1047475,00.html.

Randy Dotinga, "Stem Cells Hold Promise for Muscular Dystrophy," HealthDay, July 10, 2008. http://health.usnews.com /health-news/family-health/articles/2008/07/10/stem-cells-hold -promise-for-muscular-dystrophy.

Amanda Gardner, "Scientists Reverse Muscular Dystrophy in Mice," HealthDay, July 16, 2009. http://health.usnews.com/ health-news/family-health/articles/2009/07/16/scientists-re verse-muscular-dystrophy-in-mice.

Denise Grady, "Promising Dystrophy Drug Clears Early Test," *New York Times*, December 27, 2007. www.nytimes .com/2007/12/27/health/27drug.html.

Michael Grynbaum, "Judge Orders Drug Maker to Provide Experimental Treatment to Terminally Ill Teenager," *New York Times*, August 20, 2008. www.nytimes.com/2008/08/21 /business/21dystrophy.html?adxnnl=1&adxnn lx=1301768006 -p79r4cku3/85BUQzilGPjQ.

Nick Hanson, "Researchers Discover Chemical That May Protect Hearts of Muscular Dystrophy Patients," EurekaAlert.com, March 15, 2010. www.eurekalert.org/pub_releases/2010-03/uom -rdc031510.php.

Alice Park, "Why the Stem Cell Advance May Not Be a Breakthrough," *Time*, August 24, 2006. www.time.com/time/health /article/0,8599,1333473,00.html.

Kay Raftery, "Others Helped, So Now He Gives Back: A Cheltenham Man, Limited Physically by Muscular Dystrophy, Coaches Writers," *Philadelphia Inquirer*, April 22, 2001. http:// articles.philly.com/2001-04-22/news/25330866_1_muscular -dystrophy-tutor-graduate-student.

Shari Roan, "A Personal Fight Against a Lethal Childhood Illness," *Los Angeles Times*, May 2, 2010. www.latimes.com/news /nationworld/nation/la-sci-dystrophy-20100503,0,2995280 .story.

ScienceDaily, "New Therapy Substitutes Missing Protein in Those With Muscular Dystrophy," May 27, 2009. www.science daily.com/releases/2009/05/090526152713 .htm.

ScienceDaily, "Identification of the Gene Responsible for a New Form of Adult Muscular Dystrophy," January 22, 2010. www .sciencedaily.com/releases/2010/01/100121140338.htm.

Phil Stewart and Stephen Brown, "Italy Doctor Unplugged Euthanasia Man's Respirator," *Washington Post*, December 21, 2006. www.washingtonpost.com/wp-dyn/content/article/2006/12/21 /AR2006122100216.html.

Margaret Wahl, "DMD/BMD Drug Screen in Zebrafish Finds Three Candidates," *Quest Magazine*, March 24, 2011.

INDEX

A

Adenosine triphosphate (ATP), 57–58

African Americans, with MD, life expectancy shorter than for white MD patients, 91–94

Ataluren (PTC124)
  MD symptoms are improved with low doses of, 87–90
  trials fail to prove effectiveness in treating MD, 82–86

ATP (adenosine triphosphate), 57–58

Autoimmunity/autoimmune diseases, 79
  in T cell attack on dystrophin, 79–81

B

Becker muscular dystrophy (BMD), 10, 30
  higher prevalence of, in boys, due to X-linked condition, *94*
  incidence rate for, *70*
  prevalence in boys without family history of, 43–44
  research on creatine as treatment for, 59
  research on therapies for, 86
  symptoms of, 20
  trials of ataluren in treatment of, 84–85
  wheelchair use by boys with, by age group, *53*

Bedwell, David, 54

BMD. *See* Becker muscular dystrophy

Bush, George W., 29

C

Cancer, 69, 71

Cardiomyopathy, 20

prevalence in black *vs.* white men, 93

types of dystrophies with, 20

CDC (Centers for Disease Control and Prevention), 43, 92

Center for Developmental Biology and Perinatal Medicine (CDBPM), 38, 39

Centers for Disease Control and Prevention (CDC), 43, 92

Ciafaloni, Emma, 42, 44

CK. *See* Creatine kinase

CMD. *See* Congenital muscular dystrophy

Collins, Francis, 69

Congenital muscular dystrophy (CMD), 23, 32–33, 38

Conte, Gaetano, 12

Contractures, 18–19, 20, 21, 34
  surgery for, 26
  therapies to prevent/delay, 25

Corticosteroids, 25, 37, 57
  creatine as possible alternative to, 62–63

Creatine, *61*
  in ATP production, 57–58
  may aid in treatment of MD, 56–63

Creatine kinase (CK), 23, 104–105
  screening for, may aid in diagnosis of MD, 41–44

Cwik, Valerie, 73, 75, 80, 84

Cystic fibrosis, 52–53, 54, 55

D

DD (distal muscular dystrophy), 23, 34

Death age, median, by race/gender, 92

DeRiggi, Barbara, 52

DeRiggi, Matthew, 52, 54
Diagnosis, 23–25
Diaphragm, 19–20
Distal muscular dystrophy (DD), 23, 34
DMD. *See* Duchenne muscular dystrophy
Duchenne de Boulogne, Guillaume, 11–13, *12, 52*
Duchenne muscular dystrophy (DMD), 10, 30, 42–43, 92
  average age at diagnosis, 42
  as disease of stem cell failure, 68
  genetic mutations responsible for, 13, 53–54
  higher prevalence of, in boys, due to X-linked condition, *94*
  incidence rate for, *70*
  loss of muscle function in, *19*
  mean years of survival with/without nighttime ventilation, *85*
  percentage caused by inherited *vs.* spontaneous mutations, *78*
  prevalence in boys without family history of, 43–44
  research on creatine as treatment for, 59–62
  research on therapies for, 86
  symptoms of, 18–20
  trials of ataluren in treatment of, 84–85
  wheelchair use by boys with, by age group, *53*
DUX4 gene, 48–49, 50
Dystrophin (protein), 9, 10, *80*
  genetic mutations producing defective form of, 54
  immune reaction to, 77, 78–79
Dystrophin gene, 30, 53
  nonsense mutation in, 54
Dystrophin-glycoprotein complex, 30–31

E
EDMD. *See* Emery-Dreifuss muscular dystrophy

Electromyogram (EMG), 24
Emery-Dreifuss muscular dystrophy (EDMD), 20, 24, 34, 87
  heart involvement in, 27, 28, 38
EMG (electromyogram), 24
Exercise, role of creatine in, 58–59

F
Facioscapulohumeral muscular dystrophy (FSHD), 21–22, 32
  asymmetrical nature of, 109
  average age at onset of symptoms, by gender, *47*
  identification of genetic defect causing, 47–49
  incidence rate for, *70*
  percentage resulting from mutation in utero *vs.* inheritance, *48*
  personal account of patient receiving stem cell therapy for, 99–106
  personal account of sufferer of, 107–110
  prevalence of, 47
FDA (US Food and Drug Administration), 68
Fielding, Roger A., 56
Finkel, Richard, 52, 92, 93
Fischbach, Gerald, 66
Food and Drug Administration, US (FDA), 68
FSHD. *See* Facioscapulohumeral muscular dystrophy
Fukuyama congenital muscular dystrophy, 23

G
Gelsinger, Jesse, 67
Gene therapy, 27–28, 37
  has challenges to overcome in treatment of MD, 76–81
  for MD, first trial on human subjects, 73
  micrograph of mouse forelimb before/after treatment with, *74*

offers treatment possibilities for MD, 72–75
Genetic counseling, 28
Genetic testing, 24
Gentamicin, 25
  side effects of, 54
Genzyme Corp., 83, *83*
Gever, John, 87
Gleevec, 69
Goldstein, David, 71

H
Hare, Heather, 41
Heart problems. *See* Cardiomyopathy
Herceptin, 69
Herper, Matthew, 51

I
Innovative Therapies and Clinical Studies for Screenable Disorders (National Institute of Child Health and Human Development), 39

K
Kleve, Russ, 99
Kunkel, Louis M., 77–78
Kyphosis, 19

L
Langston, J. William, 65–66
Learning disabilities, 20
Lewis, Jerry, 97, *98*
LGMD. *See* Limb-girdle muscular dystrophy
Life expectancy
  of muscular dystrophy patients, 22
  of white MD patients is longer than for blacks, 91–94
Limb-girdle muscular dystrophy (LGMD), 32, 38
  personal account of women living with, 96–98

symptoms of, 21
trail of gene therapy for, 73–74
Louis, M., 59

M
MD. *See* Muscular dystrophy
MDA (Muscular Dystrophy Association), 13, 30, 82, 97, 98
Medications, 25
Mendel, Gregor, 13
Mendell, Jerry R., 77, 79
Miller, Langdon, 84
Miyoshi myopathy, 34
Moxley, Richard, 73–74
Muscle biopsy, 23–24
Muscular dystrophy (MD)
  cause of, 9
  incidence rate for, by type, *70*
  life expectancy of patients with, 22
  median death age in, by race/gender, 92
  national programs aim to understand/ treat, 29–40
  number of new cases annually, in US *vs.* China/India, *90*
  prognosis for, 28
  scientists are closing in on genes causing, 45–50
  types of, 18–23, 30–34
  See also Diagnosis; Symptoms; Treatment(s); *specific types*
Muscular Dystrophy Association (MDA), 13, 30, 82, 97, 98
Muscular Dystrophy Community Assistance, Research and Education Amendments (2001), 29
Myasthenia gravis, 24
Myoblast transfer, 27
Myotonic dystrophy, 22, 31–32, 38

N
National Center for Medical Rehabilitation Research (NCMRR), 38–39

National Institute of Arthritis and Musculoskeletal and Skin Diseases (NIAMS), 37–38
National Institute of Child Health and Human Development (NICHD), 38
National Institute of Neurological Disorders and Stroke (NINDS), 35–37
National Institutes of Health (NIH), 29, 84
National Registry of Myotonic and FSHD Patients and Family Members, 49
Nationwide Children's Hospital, 76
NCMRR (National Center for Medical Rehabilitation Research), 38–39
Neurology (journal), 91
New York Times (newspaper), 69
NIAMS (National Institute of Arthritis and Musculoskeletal and Skin Diseases), 37–38
NICHD (National Institute of Child Health and Human Development), 38
NIH (National Institutes of Health), 29, 84
NINDS (National Institute of Neurological Disorders and Stroke), 35–37
Nonsense mutations, 54, 55, 83
Novel Technologies in Newborn Screening (National Institute of Child Health and Human Development), 39
Nutrition, 26–27

O
Occupational therapy, 26
Oculopharyngeal dystrophy (OPMD), 22, 33–34

P
Parent Project Muscular Dystrophy, 54
Park, Madison, 91
Parkinson's disease, 65–66
Parmar, Sarabjit, 107
Pearlman, Jered P., 56

Pediatric Pharmacology Research Network, 39–40
Pediatric Scientist Training Program, 40
Pentoxifylline, 40
Physical therapy, 25–26
Prednisone, 25, 40
Prenatal diagnosis/testing, 24, 25
Protease inhibitors, 38
PTC124. *See* Ataluren
PTC Therapeutics, 52, 54, 83, 88, *89*

Q
Quercia, Nada, 15
Quest Magazine, 82

R
Research
    newborn/pediatric, 39–40
    organizations focused on, 34–35
    on therapies for DMD/BMD, 86
    on treatments for MD, 36–37
Respiratory care, 27
Rickey, Tom, 45

S
Science (journal), 46
Scoliosis, 19, 20, 26
Sex-linked diseases, 10–11, 16–18, *94*
Stem cell therapy, 38
    has not produced cures for diseases such as MD, 65–71
    personal account of MD patient going to China for, 99–106
Stillman, Bruce, 69
Surgery, 26
Sweeney, H. Lee, 54
Symptoms
    Becker muscular dystrophy, 20
    congenital muscular dystrophy, 23
    distal muscular dystrophy, 23

Duchenne muscular dystrophy, 18–20
Emery-Dreifuss muscular dystrophy, 20
facioscapulohumeral muscular
    dystrophy, 46–47
limb-girdle muscular dystrophy, 21
low doses of ataluren improve, 87–90
myotonic dystrophy, 22
oculopharyngeal dystrophy, 22
percentage of women carrying MD gene
    exhibiting/not exhibiting, *31*

T
T lymphocytes/T cell immunity, 78–81
Tapscott, Stephen, 49
Tarnopolsky, M.A., 57, 60, 62, 63
Tawil, Rabi, 48, 50, 73
Treatment(s), 25–28, 34
    drug therapy, give cautious optimism for
        MD patients, 51–55
    See also Gene therapy; Stem cell therapy

V
Van Benthuysen, Mandy, 96
Van der Maarel, Silvère, 46
Van Loon, L.J.C., 59

Vandenberghe, K., 58–59
Ventilation, nighttime, mean years of
    survival with/without, *85*

W
Walker, Christopher M., 77, 78, 79, 80–81
Walter, M.C., 59
Watson, James, 68
Women
    average age of FSHD onset in, men *vs., 47*
    median death age from MD in, by race,
        92
    muscular dystrophies in, 10
    percentage carrying MD gene exhibiting
        symptoms, *31*
    X-linked conditions and, 16–18
Wong, Brenda L.Y., 88

X
X-linked conditions, 16–18, 42, *94*
X-linked severe combined immune
    deficiency, 68

Y
Yoffe, Emily, 65